UTILITARIAN ETHICS

Utilitarian Ethics

ANTHONY QUINTON

Duckworth

Second edition published in 1989 by
Gerald Duckworth & Co. Ltd.,
The Old Piano Factory
43 Gloucester Crescent, London NW1

First edition published in 1973 by Macmillan

ISBN 0 7156 1729 X (cased)
ISBN 0 7156 1730 3 (paper)

British Library Cataloguing in Publication Data

Quinton, Anthony, *1925-*
  Utilitarian ethics. – 2nd ed
  1. Utilitarianism
  I. Title
  171'.5

ISBN 0-7156-1729-X
ISBN 0-7156-1730-3 Pbk

Printed in Great Britain by
Redwood Burn Limited, Trowbridge

CONTENTS

PREFACE TO THE SECOND EDITION

Forty years ago, when I began to study philosophy, utilitarianism seemed to be no more than an intellectual relic, a doctrine so irreversibly discredited as to be of philosophical interest only as a horrid warning. It was recognised to be historically worth studying as the theoretical foundation of much nineteenth-century reforming activity. But it was taken to have no positive message for the student of philosophy. The last major work to defend it had been Sidgwick's *Methods of Ethics*, originally published in 1874. Since then, to the extent that it had been studied at all, it was from a more or less destructively critical point of view.

The fatal blow, it seemed, had been delivered in G.E. Moore's *Principia Ethica*. There the naturalistic type of ethical theory of which utilitarianism is an instance was argued to be fallacious. Moral values, Moore held, are logically altogether disconnected from matters of natural fact that are accessible to outer or inner sense. On top of that the hedonistic identification of the good with pleasure or happiness that differentiated utilitarianism within the class of naturalistic doctrines had the arguments with which Mill had supported it undermined. Bradley had already attacked utilitarianism from another direction, more cogently than Moore, in fact. But his name had come to carry much less weight than Moore's. To some extent utilitarianism had cooperated in the business of its own demolition. Mill and Sidgwick had made damaging concessions: by way of the distinction between qualities of pleasure in Mill's case and, in Sidgwick's, by basing the principle that the general happiness is the ultimate moral end on intuition.

Mary Warnock's *Ethics since 1900*, the first post-war survey of twentieth-century British moral philosophy, which came out in 1960, confirms this claim about the derelict condition of utilitarianism both explicitly and by its choice of subjects. The moral philosophers to whom chapters are allocated are the idealist Bradley, the intuitionists Moore, Prichard and Ross, the emotivists Ayer and Stevenson, the prescriptivist Hare and the existentialist Sartre. Early in the concluding chapter, on page 197, Mary Warnock writes, of the philosophers she has considered: 'At first sight it may appear that there is one interest which all of them without exception have shared, and that is an interest in refuting Ethical Naturalism. If hostility could nullify the influence of a philosophical view, then utilitarianism ought by now to be stone dead.'

Ten years later (and two years before the first publication of this book), in W.D. Hudson's *Modern Moral Philosophy*, the list of important theorists is still much the same: Moore, Prichard and Ross, Stevenson, Hare. Like Mary Warnock, Hudson ends up discerning intimations of a revival of naturalism. She welcomed Philippa Foot's suggestion that it is not self-evident that 'empirical considerations about what does people good and what does them harm are irrelevant to deciding what is a moral principle and what is not' (op. cit., p. 205). Hudson looked with favour on what has been called the 'good reasons theory'. That theory accepts the anti-naturalist principle that moral or evaluative conclusions do not logically follow and cannot be strictly deduced from premises about matters of natural, empirical fact. But it contends that some facts at least justify or are good reasons for moral conclusions – those, namely, which concern the effects of action on happiness and suffering – while other facts are simply irrelevant to morality.

Such a position approximates to a reinstatement of utilitarianism, even if of a logically chastened kind. J.J.C. Smart, in his *Outlines of a Utilitarian System of Ethics* in 1961 (cf. chapter 5 below) circumvents anti-naturalism more boldly. Although he agrees that ultimate moral principles are not truths, or falsehoods, but matters of choice, he announces his own choice of general benevolence as a policy of action and recommends it to everyone else. In the same spirit, R.M. Hare, the most penetrating and indefatigable of the moral philosophers who hold that, as prescriptions, moral utterances are neither true nor false, and so cannot express knowledge, has come to embrace utilitarianism. At first, in *Freedom and Reason* in 1963, he was content merely to note affinities between his own view and utilitarianism. By 1976, in his important essay 'Ethical Theory and Utilitarianism' (in *Contemporary British Philosophy, Fourth Series*, ed. H.D. Lewis), these affinities had become 'close analogies', and these are further developed in his *Moral Thinking* of 1981. From the beginning Hare had always attached great importance to his thesis that the chief formal property of moral utterances is their 'universalisability'. That originally meant that every moral utterance, however singular it might look, is implicitly universal in its application. To say that I or you ought to do something amounts to saying that anyone in my or your circumstances ought to act in that way. Rather precariously, that thesis has been extended to support the proposition that in the moral point of view equal consideration should be given to the interests of all affected by the action chosen.

For utilitarianism, then, there has been a remarkable restoration of status. What had for sixty or seventy years seemed the least defensible of ethical theories found itself once more the main contestant in debate; its chief competitor being an atheoretical intuitionism which could give no better account of the counter-utilitarian principles it endorsed than their rootedness in common moral sentiment. The most surprising feature of this Cinderella-like transformation was that the most persistent and, indeed, persuasive of the exponents of the anti-naturalist principle apparently fatal for utilitarianism turned out to be its most ardent and unreserved champion.

In the last ten years, besides Hare's *Moral Thinking*, two other major utilitarian treatises have been published: R.B. Brandt's *Theory of the Good and the Right* in 1979 and James Griffin's *Well-Being* in 1986. In 1982 a long survey article, 'Modern Utilitarianism', also by James Griffin, in the *Revue Internationale de Philosophie*, no. 141, covered the preceding decade of defence and criticism of utilitarian ethics in great detail, supplying also a bibliography of 172 books and articles about it.

At the time this book was first published a utilitarian revival was beginning of which it was a small part and of which, I now see, it did not take sufficient account. I should not, for instance, have mentioned Jan Narveson's *Morality and Utility* of 1967 only in a list of books, for it was the first of the sequence of comprehensive utilitarian treatises of recent years and the most unqualified in its attempt to defend the doctrine in the traditional form given to it by Bentham and Mill (except in 'democratising' the notion of utility by defining it in terms of preferences, or expected satisfaction, rather than of actual satisfaction). As it was, the only aspect of the utilitarian revival I considered was the dispute between act and rule utilitarianism, between the idea that the right action was the one which, in its particular circumstances, would have the best results and the idea that it is the one enjoined by a rule whose general acceptance would have the best results (cf. pp. 108-10 below; also, for my own view about the topic, pp. 47-54).

That controversy has now been reconstructed by Hare into a distinction between two levels of moral thinking: the level of intuitive application in practice of habitually accepted principles and the level of critical reflection, in conditions of detachment from immediate practical problems, on the rational adequacy of the principles unreflectively accepted at the critical level.

In counting Henry Sidgwick as a critic of utilitarianism, rather than as a utilitarian, I recognised that I was defining the class of utilitarians narrowly. In view of the fact that he has become the classical ethical theorist most admired and studied by present-day moral philosophers with utilitarian sympathies, that was a decision I should not make today. Since this book was first published there has appeared, in 1977, J.B. Schneewind's excellent and extremely substantial book *Sidgwick's Ethics and Victorian Moral Philosophy*, a full study of the man, his ideas and his intellectual environment which accords to him for the first time the kind of attention which is now widely agreed to be his due.

Utilitarian Ethics is written from a position sympathetic, but not wholly committed, to utilitarianism. My principal point of disagreement is briefly mentioned on pp. 47 and 69. As I see it, morality is not concerned with the maximisation of positive well-being, utility, welfare, happiness, pleasure, desire-satisfaction or whatever, but has a negative purpose: the elimination of suffering. That negative, but still broadly utilitarian, end can be pursued by a moral agent in two ways: he can abstain from acts which would cause suffering and he can act to relieve or prevent suffering brought about the acts of others or by natural events. On that view, the promotion of positive well-being is admirable, but it is not morality. Furthermore, not causing suffering is morally compulsory in a way that the charitable relief of suffering for which one is not personally responsible is not.

Ordinary utilitarianism, along with some other moral theories and a lot of religiously inspired moral stock responses, is utopianly altruistic. It implies that in every situation in which action is possible one should choose that possibility which most augments the general welfare. That would rule out as morally wrong not only harmless self-indulgences like sitting in the sun, reading for pleasure and non-strenuous walks in the countryside (since in each case one could be working or begging for Oxfam), it would also override most of the altruistic things we do for people to whom we are bound by ties of affection. A rational morality will be finite, as well as directed towards a negative end.

This preface is not the place to develop these ideas at length. But it may be appropriate to mention briefly the way in which they either avoid or at least diminish the scale of certain persistent difficulties with which ordinary, infinite, positive utilitarianism is confronted. The ultimate end of moral action is clearly defined. Comparison between different people in respect of suffering is much less problematic than in respect of pleasure, happiness, desire-satisfaction or welfare. It largely avoids problems about maximisation of value since it does not require the elimination of suffering to be maximised. It requires one not to cause it as a matter of strict obligation and recommends one to reduce it where not caused by oneself, not to make its reduction the supreme and unremitting object of one's actions. The persistent difficulty utilitarianism has with fair or just distribution is also much watered down by this conception. It is good to relieve suffering even if the resources one puts into doing so might have been more efficiently or productively applied to starving people in Africa than to the people next door who have just come back to find their house burnt down. There is no obligation to maximise the relief of suffering in the way that there is not to cause it by one's own actions. All but a psychopathic minority of the human species want to relieve suffering. Many are in a position to do so without a degree of self-sacrifice it is unreasonable to expect. But how they do it is a matter of free moral choice.

July 1988   A.Q.

PREFACE TO THE FIRST EDITION

This exposition of utilitarian ethics is set out in a historical way. I have taken the paradigm of utilitarianism to be the ethical doctrines of Bentham and John Stuart Mill and, more specifically, I have treated as a utilitarian anyone who agrees with them that the rightness of actions is determined by the value of their consequences and that what determines the value of these consequences is the pleasure or pain that they include.

I argue, by reference to this standard, that Hume is more of a utilitarian than he is nowadays often made out to be. The same standard implies that 'ideal utilitarians' like Moore and Rashdall, who, although consequentialists, do not take pleasure or happiness as the criterion of value, are not really utilitarians at all.

The examination, criticism and, where appropriate, defence from criticism of the arguments and conclusions of Bentham and Mill has left space for no more than the barest survey of those aspects of utilitarian reasoning which most preoccupy ethical theorists at the present time, namely the structure and adequacy of consequentialist arguments in moral thinking. This is intentional and reflects my belief that the hedonistic aspect of traditional utilitarianism, its most widely repudiated ingredient, is equally deserving of consideration.

July 1972   A.Q.

INTRODUCTION

(i) DEFINITION OF UTILITARIANISM

Utilitarianism can be understood as a movement for legal, political and social reform that flourished in the first half of the nineteenth century, or, again, as the ideology of that movement. But it is also, and more persistently, a general ethical theory and it is almost exclusively in this sense that I shall be concerned with it. As a theory of ethics it provides a criterion for distinguishing between right and wrong action and, by implication, an account of the nature of the moral judgements that characterise action as right or wrong.

In its standard form it can be expressed as the combination of two principles: (1) *the consequentialist principle* that the rightness, or wrongness, of an action is determined by the goodness, or badness, of the results that flow from it and (2) *the hedonist principle* that the only thing that is good in itself is pleasure and the only thing bad in itself is pain. Utilitarians have generally taken it for granted, and have made trouble for themselves by doing so, that happiness is a sum of pleasures. Given this assumption, the doctrine can be expressed in the form of a single principle, the greatest happiness principle: *the rightness of an action is determined by its contribution to the happiness of everyone affected by it.*

This formula is, I think, a fair account of what Bentham and John Stuart Mill held to be their fundamental doctrine. Bentham says, 'By the principle of utility is meant that principle which approves or disapproves of every action whatsoever, according to the tendency which it appears to have to augment or diminish the happiness of the party whose interest is in question.'[1] The 'party in question' need not, and commonly will not, be a single person. Bentham goes on, 'An action then may be said to be conformable to the principle of utility . . . when the tendency it has to augment the happiness of the community is greater than any it has to diminish it'.[2] 'The interest of the community then is what? – the sum of the interests of the several members who compose it.'[3] There is a difference that is worth noticing between the first quotation, which speaks of what appears to contribute to the general happiness, and the second, which speaks of what actually augments or diminishes it. We shall have to inquire later which consequences of an action are relevant to its moral quality; its actual consequences, its intended consequences or the consequences it would be rational to expect from it.

John Stuart Mill says, 'The creed which accepts as the foundation of morals, Utility, or the Greatest Happiness Principle, holds that actions are right in proportion as they tend to promote happiness, wrong as they tend to produce the reverse of happiness. By happiness is intended pleasure, and the absence of pain; by unhappiness, pain, and the privation of pleasure.'[4]

There is an important moral distinction that is not explicitly provided for by the greatest happiness principle as I have formulated it, following Bentham and Mill. This is the distinction between a morally obligatory action and a morally permissible one. An obligatory action is *the* right thing to do in the circumstances, the one thing one ought to do, anything other than which it would be wrong to do. A permissible action on the other hand, is one it is quite all right to do but which is not required. An obligatory action is something it would be *wrong not* to do; a permissible action is one it would be *not wrong* to do.

Bentham is aware of this distinction but seems to think that it is of no importance. He says, 'Of an action that is conformable to the principle of utility one may always say either that it is one that ought to be done, or at least that it is not one that ought not to be done. One may say also, that it is right it should be done; at least that it is not wrong it should be done; that it is a right action; at least that it is not a wrong action.'[5]

What Bentham seems to be suggesting is that any action that detracts from the general happiness is wrong, it ought not to be done; while any action that adds to it is all right or permissible, but is not something that ought to be done, is not something obligatory. On this interpretation is any account possible of what positively ought to be done? The crucial point is that action is always the outcome of a selection between possible alternatives, at least if it is the kind of action to which moral judgement is appropriate. Now any possible action which would detract from the general happiness is wrong and therefore ought not to be done; it is obligatory to abstain from it, to do something else. If there are several other possibilities, all of them happiness-augmenting, it is obligatory to do one of them, but not any particular one of them rather than any other. Only if there is just one alternative possibility that augments happiness will it be obligatory.

But this produces certain problems. First, it is possible that all the available alternatives would detract from the general happiness to some extent. It would seem congruous with the spirit of the general happiness principle to choose that action which detracts least from it. But this yields a paradox: as detracting from the general happiness it ought not to be done, as detracting less than any other possibility it ought to be done. A way out of this difficulty, expounded, for example, with great laboriousness in G. E. Moore's *Ethics*, is to say that one ought in any situation to choose that alternative which contributes most or, if that is the way things are, detracts least from the general happiness. But this has the disconcerting consequence that in every situation there is one thing which it is obligatory to do and all other alternatives are wrong. Furthermore it is probably very rare for people's actions to be the *best possible* thing to do in the circumstances. So people nearly always act wrongly. I shall return to this later.

A second difficulty arises from inaction. Doing nothing at all is generally one of the possibilities open to an agent. But one who does nothing does not positively detract from the general happiness. Does it follow that inaction is never wrong? Often it is an alternative to a possible action which would greatly increase the general happiness or, an even more important case, which would greatly diminish general suffering. This again suggests that actions are not right or wrong absolutely, that is considered only with respect to their own consequences alone, but that their moral quality is a comparative matter, determined by the difference between their consequences, good or bad, and the consequences of the available alternatives. Most contemporary utilitarians, in the light of these difficulties, follow Moore in formulating the first principle of the doctrine in a comparative, rather than an absolute way.

There is a terminological point that needs to be made. There are many ethical theorists who accept the consequentialist theory of obligation advanced by standard utilitarianism but reject its hedonist theory of value. Either, like Moore, they think that the principal possessors of intrinsic value are quite distinct from pleasure (in Moore's case pre-eminent intrinsic value is ascribed to affectionate personal relations and the contemplation of beauty) or, like Rashdall, they take pleasure to be one intrinsically valuable thing amongst others, for example, virtue, knowledge, beauty. This type of view is often called *ideal* utilitarianism, in contrast to the *hedonistic* utilitarianism of Bentham and, with qualifications, of John Stuart Mill. When I refer to utilitarianism without explicit qualification it will always be to its standard hedonistic form.

Before leaving this matter of definition it may be useful to summarise three respects in which the classic formulations of utilitarianism are in need of clarification. First, there is the problem of deciding which consequences are relevant: *actual*, *intended* or *rationally expectable*. Secondly, there is the problem of deciding whether the consequences of an action should be assessed *absolutely* or *by comparison* with the consequence of available alternatives. Thirdly, there is the problem of deciding whether obligation should be defined *positively*, in terms of the maximisation of happiness, or *negatively*, in terms of the minimisation of suffering. These issues will be discussed further as will the problems arising about the precise interpretation of the

4

hedonist principle, in particular that of the supposed identity of happiness (or welfare) with a sum of pleasures.

The classic utilitarians, like most ethical theorists before the twentieth century, took it for granted that moral judgements are genuine statements, true or false. Furthermore they took them to be statements of ordinary natural fact. The primary judgements of value they saw as introspective reports of experienced pleasure or pain. From these could be derived the judgements about the happiness or suffering of people in general on which judgements of obligation should be based, these judgements of obligation being themselves causal propositions of a rather complicated kind.

A leading theme of moral philosophy in this century has been that any such naturalistic account of moral convictions and affirmations, which treats them as statements of empirical fact, must be mistaken. In its developed form this doctrine of anti-naturalism argues from the fact that moral judgements are practical in a certain way, that they constitute sufficient reasons for action without additional assumptions, for example about the agent's wants or tastes or purposes, that they cannot be statements but must be imperatives or proposals or the announcements of decisions. However, there are convinced anti-naturalists who would still describe themselves as utilitarians but, as it might be put, of a *normative* kind. For them the utilitarian principle is not a fundamental moral truth, or truth about morality, but rather a basic moral choice or commitment which they are prepared to make and which they recommend to others. J. J. C. Smart's version of this procedure will be examined later.

(ii) EGOISM, MOTIVATION AND THE HARMONY OF INTERESTS

The famous first three sentences of Bentham's *Principles of Morals and Legislation* join together two things whose intimate involvement with each other has been at once a central feature of utilitarianism and a source of much confusion. 'Nature', Bentham says, 'has placed mankind under the governance of two

5

sovereign masters, *pain* and *pleasure*. It is for them alone to point out what we ought to do, as well as to determine what we shall do. On the one hand the standard of right and wrong, on the other the chain of causes and effects, are fastened to their throne.'[6] Bentham, in effect, asserts both utilitarianism, which states that men ought to aim at the general happiness, and egoism, which states that in actual fact men always aim at their own happiness. His utilitarianism is an ethical theory; his egoism a psychological one.

What is more, the closely intertwined way in which he presents the two doctrines implies that there is some connection between them. This implication is drawn out in Mill's notorious proof, or 'proof', of the utilitarian principle, one of whose premises is 'that there is in reality nothing desired except happiness'[7] or that 'happiness is the sole end of human action'.[8]

Critics have often argued that these two doctrines are in some way inconsistent. It is obvious enough that they are not directly incompatible, since one of them says how men in fact behave, the other how they should. But it is commonly supposed that it cannot be the case that a man ought to do something unless he can do it. Thus if he can aim only at his own happiness it cannot be the case that he ought to aim at the general happiness.

This argument would be valid if it could be assumed that the general happiness and the agent's own happiness are distinct. But can this assumption be made? There is an *ad hominem* argument that might be used to justify it. Utilitarians have often said that each man is the best judge of what his own happiness consists in. But it seems manifest that men often act in ways that do not promote the general happiness, or do not promote it as much as some possible alternative action they might have done. But, if psychological egoism is true, the way in which they act shows what they take their happiness to consist in and this is often in conflict with the promotion of the general happiness.

To be consistent, then, the utilitarian who is also a psychological egoist must say that the set of alternative actions open to an agent in given circumstances is not limited, by the egoist prin-

6

ciple, to that single action which he believes will contribute most to his own happiness. And this, in fact, they usually do. For them what an agent *can* do, in the sense required for it to be the case that he ought to do it, is what he could be induced to do by sanctions. These sanctions should ideally conform to the principle of utility by contributing more to the general happiness than they detract from it. The sanctions in question must be efficient, in that they really would induce the agent to act in the required way, and economical, in that the contribution to the general happiness made by the action they produce outweighs the suffering endured by the agent from the sanctions or the threat of them. There are many things, other than what an agent in fact does, that he could do, on the principle that one can do what one can be got to do. But this ideal alternative is the morally relevant one.

In general, utilitarians claim that there is a *natural harmony of interests*. By this they mean that action aimed at the general happiness will in fact most fully realise the agent's own happiness. To the extent that this is true, or more precisely that there is good reason to believe it, a rational agent will, in pursuing the general happiness, follow the most rational policy for the achievement of his own greatest happiness. But this natural harmony of interests is not something that will be consummated if men are left to act as they choose, without guidance or interference from outside, because men are not all rational and perhaps none are wholly rational. A system of sanctions needs to be instituted which, by making action that is unpropitious for the general happiness obviously damaging to the agent's own happiness, brings about an *artificial harmony of interests*.

Bentham, indeed, enumerated three sanctions over and above the 'physical sanction' which is the pain or pleasure resulting from an action by purely natural causes and independent of any exercise of the human, or divine, will. There is the political sanction, applied by the state under its laws; the moral sanction, applied informally by the community in accordance with its moral convictions; and the religious sanction, applied by God in the form of eternal rewards and punishments. But law was the device for bringing about an artificial harmony of interests with which he was most concerned. J. S. Mill added to these the 'internal' sanction of conscience.

The idea of a natural harmony of interests was inspired by the classical economic theory of Adam Smith which argued that the greatest economic advantage to all would accrue from the unremitting and wholly rational pursuit by each of his own economic advantage. (A remoter source is Mandeville's affectedly 'wicked' thesis that private vices yield public benefits.) But even this natural harmony of economic interests presupposes the complete rationality of men's economic behaviour. Although not true it is less obviously false than the wider assumption that men's behaviour in general is completely rational.

There is, it is held, then, an ultimate natural harmony of interests. The pursuit of the general happiness is what would in fact most promote the happiness of individual men and, if they were wholly rational, that is what they would pursue. But they are not. They aim at what they mistakenly think will yield their own greatest happiness. It is easier to get them to act rightly by altering the probable short-run consequences of their actions, by attaching legal and other sanctions to the undesirable actions they are prone to do, than to get them to realise their mistakes about the long-run consequences of their actions for their own happiness.

Is there any such ultimate natural harmony of interests? It seems unlikely. Of course the happiness of some people, those I love, is a constitutive part of my own happiness. If everybody loved his neighbour as himself, general and particular happiness would coincide. Furthermore, the happiness of some people is a causally necessary condition of my own happiness in various ways. I am unlikely to be happy in a society of miserable and desperate people and I am certainly going to be unhappy in a society whose members have identified me as the cause of their unhappiness. 'Revenge', as Hobbes remarked, 'is a kind of wild justice', a human, but nonetheless natural device for bringing about a harmony of interests.

What this shows is that I have a direct interest in the happiness of the people I love (who are likely to be a rather small part of the human race as a whole), a moderate indirect interest in the non-misery of people whose misery might have a bad effect on my own happiness (which nowadays, at any rate, covers the entire human race) and a rather stronger interest in not causing misery to people who might take revenge on me. In fact every sane, morally adult person has other motives than these for avoiding action, however attractive in other respects, that would cause suffering to others and again for performing actions, otherwise unattractive, that would contribute to the general happiness. For one thing, our moral education makes us capable of being disgusted with ourselves.

These considerations clearly show that there is no direct conflict between a man's own happiness and the general happiness, no necessary opposition between them. It shows, indeed, that some concern for the general happiness is essential to the pursuit of one's own happiness, either as a constitutive part of it or as its causal condition. But they fall well short of showing that the pursuit of the general happiness and the fully rational pursuit of one's own happiness are identical. At most, given one man's dependence on and vulnerability to other men, it is a necessary condition of the achievement of his own happiness and the avoidance of suffering that he should not cause gross suffering in others and that he should do something to relieve suffering that is not of his making. This provides some sort of answer to the question 'why should I be moral?' but not, perhaps, to the question 'why should I be as enthusiastically moral and self-sacrificing as classical utilitarianism enjoins me to be?'

Now it could be argued that no ethical theory is complete until it does answer this question, in the sense of 'moral' appropriate to it. But if the utilitarian answer is less than fully convincing this is not a weakness peculiar to it. The main point of this section has been to show that there is at any rate no inconsistency between utilitarianism and the psychological egoism with which it has usually been associated. If men do always aim at their own happiness it does not follow that they cannot aim at the general happiness. Men can act otherwise than they do, in the utilitarian view, because they can be induced to act differently in an acceptable way. Furthermore, even if not clearly identical with the greatest happiness of each individual, the general happiness is to some extent a constituent and to some extent a causally necessary condition of individual happiness.

I. THE PRECURSORS OF UTILITARIANISM

(i) ETHICS BEFORE UTILITARIANISM

Both of the essential constituents of utilitarianism, as I have defined it, hedonism and consequentialism, are present in Greek ethics. But there is still something crucial missing. This is the element of universality, the insistence of standard utilitarianism that it is the *general* happiness that is the criterion of right conduct. The reason for this omission is the way in which the philosophers of ancient Greece conceived the central ethical problem. For them the question 'how should I live?' took what to us seems a fundamentally prudential or self-regarding form. It amounted for them to an inquiry as to how a man could secure *his own* happiness, fulfilment or perfection. Benevolence, altruism, philanthropy, a concern for the happiness of others occupied a secondary, and even marginal, position in their ethical recommendations. It was not conceived as an end in itself but rather as a means to, or a condition of, the self-realisation of the individual. Greek philosophers in general, and Plato and Aristotle in particular, found a place for restricted benevolence by emphasising the role of friendship in a fully satisfying life and Aristotle made a somewhat disdainful 'liberality' part of his conception of the ethically ideal or 'magnanimous' man. But it was Christianity that first established an essential connection between morality and the happiness or well-being of humanity at large.

In developing their more or less prudential life-styles the Greek moralists unreflectively assumed a consequentialist position. The only way in which they conceived it to be possible to justify a type of conduct was by reference to the results to which it gave rise, for the agent, of course. Many of them were hedonists. Aristippus of Cyrene, indeed, was a hedonist in the colloquial sense, urging the pre-eminent claims of bodily pleasure as an end, in view of its greater intensity. But more commonly, as with Democritus, it would appear, and above all Epicurus, a distinction was drawn between the more intense but also more turbulent pleasures of the body and the calmer but ultimately more satisfying pleasures of the mind. This distinction between lower and higher pleasures was to be revived by John Stuart Mill as one of the most disputed elements in his exposition of utilitarianism.

Others, the Cynics and Stoics, in effect denied the utilitarian identification of happiness with a sum of pleasures. Taking the achievement of happiness as the ultimate justifying end of conduct, they believed the surest way to it to be the suppression of desire and, as a result, indifference to the ordinary sources of pleasure. Plato shared this asceticism but his point of view was less negative. The point of freeing oneself from the solicitations of ordinary desire was not, for him, the attainment of a merely passive condition of peace of mind but rather to clear the ground for the highest satisfaction possible to men, the rational contemplation which is fulfilled by the achievement of wisdom, the most elevated of the virtues.

With Christianity morality came to be endowed with what for us is its essential content, a concern for others. But in two absolutely fundamental respects this altruism was unutilitarian. In the first place, its conception of the happiness or well-being of mankind was ascetical and non-hedonistic. Men are morally required not to injure others, but this is to be achieved at least as much by denying them pleasures in the ordinary sense as it is by supplying them with them. Man's greatest felicity is the beatific vision of God that is to be enjoyed after bodily death by those who have been saved. It follows that the greatest kindness one man can do to another is to work for his salvation and that will generally mean to detach him from the natural earthly satisfactions. In the extreme case of the obstinately heretical the achievement of salvation may require the ultimate bodily suffering of being burnt at the stake. Nevertheless the Christian obligation of charity was not as indifferent to natural, bodily wants and needs as this might suggest. It called for the relief of those afflicted by hunger and sickness. But if the diminution of pain and the provision of pleasure, in a fairly elevated sense, are not altogether ignored by Christian morality, it conceives them as secondary, and, indeed, comparatively trivial, ends of conduct.

The second highly unutilitarian feature of Christian ethics is the account it gives of moral knowledge, of the way in which the principles of right conduct are discovered. In its simplest and most rudimentary form it bases the validity of the moral principles it enjoins on the fact that they are the commands of God. That God will reward or punish me eternally for complying with or disobeying his commands is an adequate, though not ideally estimable, motive for obeying them. But it is not this consequential property that makes them obligatory.

Some Christian theologians, conspicuously Aquinas, mitigated the irrational authoritarianism of this doctrine by maintaining that at least the demands of morality that were not specifically religious were discoverable by the natural reason of man. Several considerations lay behind this. It seemed intolerable to suppose that everyone who was ignorant, because of the time or place at which he lived, of the Christian revelation, its scriptural record and its authoritative interpreter, the Church, must on that account be altogether without knowledge of morality. Secondly, the external means by which God's commands are communicated to men are liable to various kinds of failure and even corruption. The moral content of the Bible requires interpretation and its official interpreters may be misguided or even morally deficient.

Although some, like Duns Scotus and William of Ockham, held that right actions are right because God commands them and that if his commands had been quite different from what they are they would still have been right, the more usual view was that God, being by definition good, is logically constrained to will what is right. An essential aspect of God's goodness indeed, is his benevolence, his desire for the happiness of his creatures. But this does not imply a utilitarian morality since God's conception of what the true happiness of his creatures consists in is more authoritative than their own, and differs from what they are naturally inclined to suppose.

The prevailing account of moral knowledge that emerged from the developed Christian theology of the late middle ages was rationalistic. It maintained that the basic principles of right conduct owe their authority to the fact that they are divine commands. God has provided two ways in which they can be discovered: externally in scripture, whether interpreted by the church or the individual believer, and internally, by an innate capacity for apprehending the self-evident truth of the principles in question, a moral reason analogous to the reason by which men apprehend the fundamental truths of mathematics. Aquinas's doctrine of natural law was conveyed by way of Hooker to Locke, who explicitly associates morality with mathematics and the existence of God as items of demonstrative knowledge. In the ethics of Samuel Clarke and Richard Price this ethical rationalism, which understands the moral quality of a kind of action as intrinsic to it, as being logically essential to it in the way that three-sidedness is to a triangle, is altogether detached from revelation and advanced as an autonomous and sufficient explanation of our knowledge of morality. Clarke elaborates the comparison of moral with mathematical knowledge (which Locke had only outlined in general terms, and very unconvincingly illustrated) speaking of the obligatoriness of an action as an abstract relation of fittingness between it and its circumstances, in precise analogy with the abstract relations studied by the geometer.

Christian ethics, then, and the kind of ethical rationalism that emerged from it to become the prevailing theory of moral knowledge in the seventeenth and eighteenth centuries, fostered an account of the *content* of morality as altruistic and benevolent which was to be central to utilitarianism. But their account of the nature of the general well-being at which right conduct should aim was non-hedonistic. Furthermore the rightness of a type of conduct was not to be inferred from the generally beneficial consequences to which it would give rise. Rather, true benevolence was defined in terms of the intrinsic and rationally self-evident rightness of actions.

(ii) UTILITARIANISM EMERGES

Classical utilitarianism is a secular and naturalistic doctrine. It conceives morality as an institution designed to harmonise the conduct and satisfactions of men on earth and takes the correct method of acquiring moral knowledge to be empirical. It might, then, seem reasonable to expect that an explicitly utilitarian ethical theory would emerge with the development of a systematic secular naturalism in philosophy in general. The philosophy of Hobbes was such a system, the first and most closely-knit of the modern age, yet Hobbes was not a utilitarian, indeed he was not, except in a very marginal sense, a hedonist. The starting-point of his ethics is a firmly, even brutally, egoistic theory of human motivation. The universal end of men's actions is the satisfaction of their desires. But there is one object of desire to which men will, if rational, give an absolute pre-eminence, self-preservation, or more precisely, the avoidance of violent death at the hands of other men. No very clear reason is given for according this primacy to self-preservation. Hobbes holds that pleasure is the natural accompaniment of those impacts of the external world on the human organism which are propitious to its continued vitality and that pleasure is a determinant of desire. This might seem to suggest that the real point or purpose of the appetitive side of human nature is self-preservation. Again the satisfaction of the desire for continued life is a condition of the satisfaction of any other desire. (But that form of reasoning would prove that salt, since it is indispensable to our diet, is an ideal diet on its own.)

Rational reflection shows that, since every man is vulnerable to every other, security from violent death can be established only by the acceptance and enforcement of a system of rules that require men to abstain from injuring each other. All have an equal interest in the operation of such a system of rules. It is rational to comply with such rules only if they are generally enforced and they can be enforced only if they are generally accepted. In this theory morality dissolves into law and the obligation to obey the law is strictly self-regarding and prudential.

Hobbes is often described as a subjectivist and he does say that men *call* good whatever is the object of their desire.[9] But what he believes really is good is self-preservation and, although one man's preservation is distinct from another's, the rationally discoverable condition of these various singular self-preservations is general: an effectively enforced system of laws requiring abstention from mutual injury. The ultimate justifying end of obligation then is egoistic; only its indispensable condition is general and this derivative end is a means not to happiness but to survival.

But although Hobbes was not a utilitarian his ethical views did evoke the first clearly utilitarian account of morality, that of Richard Cumberland, whose *De Legibus Naturae* was published in 1672. Although a bishop and primarily concerned to refute Hobbes, Cumberland, for sound polemical reasons, chose to argue his case as much as possible in Hobbes's grimly economical terms. He agrees with Hobbes that the laws of nature, in other words the general principles of morality, need explanation and are not adequately justified by the theories which see them as divine commands or self-evident truths. They are means to an end, in particular the 'joint felicity of all rationals', 'the aggregate or sum of all those good things which either we can contribute towards, or are necessary to, the happiness of all rational beings, considered as collected into one body'. Right action, he says, is 'the endeavour, to the utmost of our power, of promoting the common good of the whole system of rational agents' and it conduces 'to the good of every part, in which our own happiness, as that of a part, is contained'.[10]

Apart from making the general happiness, rather than the, inevitably general, preservation of life, the ultimate moral end, Cumberland's main difference from Hobbes lies in the account he gives of human motivation. Human nature is not as destructively egoistic as Hobbes makes it out to be; benevolence is as much a part of it as naked self-interest. It was this project of undermining Hobbes's egoistic theory of motivation which was to dominate the ethical thinking of the subsequent century. Hobbes's challenge to conventional morality did not attack its content but the basis of its claim on us. It did not cast doubt on the received ideas about what we ought to do but only on the usual account of why we ought to do it. Thus, in the moral sense theories of Shaftesbury and Hutcheson, the problem of the criterion of right conduct occupies a small place. There is a general assumption of the identity of virtue and benevolence and Hutcheson actually uses the phrase 'the greatest happiness of the greatest number'. But the main emphasis is laid on the springs of benevolent action in the social nature of man. The content of morality became problematic only with the decay of Christian belief, which had hitherto ensured a fair measure of moral uniformity, together with increasing knowledge of the deviant moral convictions and practices of remote peoples.

(iii) HUME

By far the most important, elaborate and philosophically penetrating anticipation of the utilitarianism of Bentham and Mill is to be found in the ethical writings of David Hume; Book 3 of the *Treatise of Human Nature* (1740) and the *Enquiry Concerning the Principles of Morals* (1751). Cumberland's purpose had been polemical rather than constructive; he was an ungainly writer and a very imperfect expositor. Something very like the greatest happiness principle does indeed figure in his book as the ultimate standard for the justification of specific moral principles. But it is only one feature in a doctrine which embodies numerous non-utilitarian elements; for example, a conception of the general good in terms of perfection almost as much as in terms of happiness and the acceptance of a religious foundation for morality. At all levels Hume's approximation to utilitarianism proper is much closer: he conceives morality in a wholly secular way and, more superficially, there is constant explicit mention of utility.

Nevertheless Hume is not quite a utilitarian. In the first place he does not conceive it to be his task as a moral philosopher to consider the way in which moral beliefs are to be justified so much as to explain causally how they come to be made and how they work. Morality for Hume is a phenomenon which is to be investigated in the spirit of the sub-title of his *Treatise*: 'An Attempt to Introduce the Experimental Method of Reasoning into Moral Subjects'. But here, as elsewhere in Hume's philosophy, what is presented as the outcome of a causal inquiry is readily available for reinterpretation as an analysis or a criterion of validity. Hume explains causal belief as the result of the workings of constant conjunction on the mind by way of the principle of the association of ideas. This is easily converted into the regularity theory, which analyses assertions to the effect that one event is the cause of another as implicitly general statements about the regularity with which events like the first are followed by neighbouring events like the second. (Indeed Hume himself at times defines causation in this way.) Again Hume explains our belief in the existence of material objects, which are continuous and distinct from us, in a way that our impressions of them are not, as the causal outcome of the characteristic constancy and coherence of the sequence of our impressions. It is a short step from that to the phenomenalism which *defines* a material object as a systematic, or 'constant and coherent', array of actual and possible impressions of the senses.

A second and, to many contemporary ethical theorists, more substantial deviation from utilitarianism in Hume is his uniquely serious realisation, as compared with all moral philosophers until very recent times, of the essentially practical nature of moral judgements. 'Morals', he insists at the beginning of his discussion, 'have an influence on the actions and affections', they 'excite passions, and produce or prevent actions'.[11] His position is expressed in a famous quotation that has served as the motto of much recent ethics: 'In every system of morality, which I have hitherto met with, I have always remarked, that the author proceeds for some time in the ordinary way of reasoning, and establishes the being of a God, or makes observations concerning human affairs; when of a sudden I am surprised to find, that instead of the usual copulations of propositions, *is*, and *is not*, I meet with no proposition that is not connected with an *ought*, or an *ought not*. This change is imperceptible; but is, however, of the last consequence. For as this *ought*, or *ought not*, expresses some new relation or affirmation, it is necessary that it should be observed and explained; and at the same time that a reason should be given, for what seems altogether inconceivable, how this new relation can be a deduction from others, which are entirely different from it.'[12]

This, in the view of many interpreters, seems to amount to the recently popular conviction that moral judgements are logically unique and autonomous. The interpretation is supported by Hume's denial that 'moral distinctions' are derived from either reason or the senses and by his insistence on the practical nature of moral judgements which is what is usually invoked to explain their logical uniqueness and autonomy.

Hume rejects ethical rationalism of the kind hinted at by Locke and developed by Clarke. Equally he maintains that the moral qualities of actions are no more matters of fact perceptible by the senses than they are abstract 'fitnesses' apprehensible by the understanding. 'Take any action allowed to be vicious: wilful murder, for instance. Examine it in all lights, and see if you can find that matter of fact, or real existence, which you call *vice*. In whichever way you take it, you find only certain passions, motives, volitions and thoughts. There is no other matter of fact in the case. The vice entirely escapes you, as long as you consider the object. You can never find it, till you turn your reflexion into your own breast, and find a sentiment of disapprobation, which arises in you, towards this action. Here is a matter of fact; but it is the object of feeling, not of reason. It lies in yourself, not in the object.'[13] But the moral judgement is not a report or description of this sentiment or emotion. 'To have the sense of virtue, is nothing but to *feel* a satisfaction of a particular kind from the contemplation of a character. The very *feeling* constitutes our praise or admiration. . . . We do not infer a character to be virtuous, because it pleases: but in feeling that it pleases after such a particular manner, we in effect feel that it is virtuous.'[14]

Moral judgements, then, are neither necessary truths, demonstrable by reason, nor descriptions of external matters of fact. They are the unreflective expressions of a particular kind of inward sentiment or emotion, that of approbation or its opposite. From this point on it is Hume's task to explain how and in what circumstances the characteristically moral emotion, the pleasure of approval or the pain of disapproval, is brought about. His answer is that approval is caused by our awareness that actions and characters are either agreeable or useful to ourselves or to others, in other words afford pleasure or the means to it to someone.

This conclusion poses the favourite ethical problem of the age, in the form in which Hume confronts it: that which concerns the appeal to an individual of what contributes to the happiness of others. Why should I be pleased by the disinterested contemplation of the happiness of another, especially to the extent of being led thereby, at some cost to myself, to promote it? Hume's answer is in three parts. First, men are all naturally benevolent, even if only to a mild extent and towards a restricted circle of people. 'There is no such passion in human minds, as the love of mankind, merely as such';[15] but equally there is no such thing as absolute, disinterested malevolence. Secondly, there is sympathy, the tendency, based associatively on the similarity of other men to ourselves, to feel pleased and pained when they do, even if less intensely. 'When I see the *effects* of passion in the voice and gesture of any person, my mind immediately passes from these effects to their causes, and forms such a lively idea of the passion, as is presently converted into the passion itself.'[16] Finally, Hume alleges, the limited, parochial tendency of benevolence and sympathy is corrected to provide for the necessities of communication. 'It is impossible that we could ever converse together on any reasonable terms, were each of us to consider characters and persons, only as they appear from his particular point of view.'[17]

For these three reasons, then, men are prone to submit the actions and characters of themselves and others to *disinterested* contemplation. If what they contemplate is agreeable or useful to anyone, is pleasant or a means to pleasure, it arouses in the contemplators sentiments of approval, which are verbally expressed in moral judgements and practically expressed in conduct. Hume presents this thesis as a causal law of human psychology. But it is easily converted into an ethical theory proper, into an account of the criteria of validity of moral judgements. If what we *believe* to be agreeable or useful is what we *judge* to be right, it is natural to conclude that what *really is* agreeable or useful really is right.

This closely related, and genuinely utilitarian, position, to which Hume approximates in his general observations about morality, is something to which he comes even closer in his account of the part of commonly accepted morality to which he devotes the most detailed attention: the requirements of justice. Justice, which Hume curiously identifies with respect for the rights of property, is described, together with promise-keeping and obedience to law and the state, as an artificial virtue, in contrast to the natural virtue of benevolence. What makes justice and the other virtues like it artificial is the fact that there is no instinctive impulse in men to act in accordance with its dictates, whereas there is such a natural impulse, even if not a very powerful one, to benevolence.

Hume's distinction between natural and artificial virtue is not very precise but it is essentially that while the utility of benevolence is obvious (it is in fact truistic), that of justice can be recognised only as the result of more or less complicated reasoning. Hume speaks of property, promises, and the state as conventions, and this suggests a possibly better way of drawing the distinction he has in mind, one that has affinities to Hobbes's account of the necessity for generally applicable rules of conduct. Benevolence, provided it is not accompanied by gross misinformation about the incidence of happiness and suffering, is guaranteed to promote utility. But the artificial virtues promote utility only if they are fairly generally followed. Property, promises, and the state are institutions which it is useful to respect only if they are generally respected. It is the utility of the institution, of the general rules that it embodies, that explains why it is right to act in accordance with such institutional rules in particular cases where the immediate consequences of doing so are of negligible or even negative utility.

In general, Hume takes men's propensities towards approval and disapproval as given. His aim is to explain them, not to justify or criticise them. Yet his own rejection of religion has obvious critical implications for conventional morality. If there is no God, and no life after death for him to reward or punish us in, this must have a bearing on the utility of our actions. Bentham acknowledged a great indebtedness to Hume but he put his ethical inheritance to critical uses that formed no part of the intentions of his benefactor. Where Hume sought to show that ordinary, unreflective morality has a rational foundation of which men are largely unaware, Bentham put this rational foundation to work as an instrument for the radical criticism and reformation of ordinary morality.

In this critical and reformist use of the principle of utility, Bentham was anticipated and influenced by two European students of Hume: Helvétius and Beccaria. The main topic of Helvétius's *De L'Esprit* (1758), is an account of human nature as an associatively developed system of sensations, including pleasure and pain, from which he derived the conclusion that men are unrestrictedly malleable by education and law. 'L'éducation peut tout.' Men can be made to do almost anything by appropriate modification of their environment and experience. The question arises: in what direction should they be influenced? Helvétius took it as beyond question that this aim should be public utility, the general interest, the general happiness.

Beccaria, in his highly influential essay *Dei Delitti e delle Pene*

(1764), applied the criterion of utility in an account of the nature of a rational system of judicial punishment which consciously deviates in numerous respects from the accepted judicial practices of his age. 'In order for punishment not to be, in every instance, an act of violence of one or of many against a private citizen, it must be essentially public, prompt, necessary, the least possible in the given circumstances, proportionate to the crimes, dictated by the laws.'[18] All the properties that the principle of utility recommends here for punishment were more or less conspicuously absent from the actual administration of the sanctions of the law.

Hume was by no means the only conservative utilitarian. Paley, for example, found utilitarian justifications for all the details of the established order. What is singular about Hume's position is that he is at once conservative and anti-religious. As a patriotic Scotsman Hume was inevitably hostile to the Whig oppressors of his country. A more direct and theoretical reason for his conservative point of view is his pervading scepticism and his associated respect for whatever is customary: 'Men generally fix their affections more on what they are possessed of, than on what they never enjoyed: for this reason, it would be greater cruelty to dispossess a man of any thing, than not to give it him.'[19] This absence of a critical impulse towards ideas and institutions, provided always that they are not religious, is congruous with his consistent preference for an explanatory over a justificatory approach to morality.

(iv) THEOLOGICAL UTILITARIANISM

In 1731 John Gay published, anonymously, his *Preliminary Dissertation* to a work by somebody else on the origin of evil. Despite the furtiveness of its presentation to the world, Gay's utilitarianism was much less entwined with extraneous matter than Cumberland's and much less complicated and idiosyncratic than Hume's. Gay defined virtue as 'conformity to a rule of life directing the action of all rational creatures with respect to each other's happiness'.[20] His starting-point was a straightforward

23

acceptance of the essential benevolence of God. Since God, by his very nature, must will the happiness of his creatures, it follows that we must discover what his will is, and thus what is morally required of us, by determining what actions promote the happiness of mankind. The happiness of mankind, in other words, is the criterion of the will of God.

As well as validating or authorising the principle of utility, God, according to Gay, also provides us with a sufficient motive for conforming our actions to it. Gay defines obligation in a Hobbesian, seemingly non-moral and misleading way as 'the necessity of doing or omitting an action in order to be happy'.[21] This comes near to assimilating the sense of obligation relevant to morality to that in which we commonly speak of, for example, being obliged to let go of something that is too heavy to hold. What is misleading about this, in the particular context of Gay's theory, is that while an action is held to be *right* if it contributes to the happiness of all, it is obligatory only if it contributes to the happiness of the agent. Right and obligatory action, which for us are much the same thing, are thus conceived as logically distinct. They coincide in fact only by way of the benevolence of God, who adjusts the sanctions of conduct so as to make the pursuit of the general happiness by each agent the best, or only, way to secure his own happiness.

In the course of his discussion Gay anticipates Bentham's four sanctions of morality in precise detail. He distinguishes natural, virtuous, civil and religious sanctions; a classificatory scheme to which Bentham was to make only verbal alterations. Furthermore Gay anticipates Bentham's clear-cut and simplified view that happiness is a sum of pleasures, between which the only relevant distinctions are quantitative. This is the presupposition of Bentham's hedonic calculus which explains the respects in which pleasure is to be measured and how the results of these measurements are to be summed.

Abraham Tucker, in his *Light of Nature Pursued* (1768), a vast, diffuse work at the opposite literary extreme from Gay's brief, consecutive essay, presents essentially the same body of ideas.

He follows Hartley in pointing out that there are good utilitarian reasons for guiding action by general rules, rather than working out the consequences of each proposed action. We often need to make moral decisions quickly and adherence to general rules worked out in an impersonal way is a safeguard against any tendency to self-regarding miscalculation in cases where our own interests are involved. He differs from Gay, and even more from Bentham, in holding that the computation of the amount of value to be realised by action must be impressionistic, not mechanically arithmetical.

Tucker's manner of writing ensured that he would be read very little. It was left to William Paley, a most lucid and elegant expositor, to express his and Gay's ideas in a sufficiently attractive way to make them really influential. For many years this influence was institutionalised, so to speak, by the fact that Paley's *Principles of Moral and Political Philosophy* (1785) was the official medium of ethical instruction at Cambridge. He added little to what he acquired from Gay and Tucker. With them he holds the general happiness to be the *summum bonum*, he regards happiness as a sum of pleasures that differ relevantly only in quantity, and he maintains that God must, as it were by definition, desire the happiness of mankind and takes the sanctions of eternal reward and punishment through which God seeks to realise this end as providing the only rational motive for morally correct conduct. His main contribution to theological utilitarianism is a certain ingenuous openness which often amounts to simple blatancy, as in the famous definition of virtue as 'the doing good to mankind, in obedience to the will of God, for the sake of everlasting happiness'.[22] Bentham had a substantial measure of Paley's self-confident naïveté. He follows Paley in rejecting the moral sense or intuitionist alternatives to utilitarianism as arbitrary and irrational. The chief ethical difference between them is that Bentham provides a very different account of moral motivation. There is also a more practical or ideological difference. Paley invoked the general happiness principle to endorse the practices and institutions of the *status quo* while Bentham invoked it to make something very like a clean sweep of them. This flat opposition suggests that agreement that the pleasure or happiness of all is the *summum bonum* is no guarantee of the settlement of disputes about specific moral and political issues. The conditions of the general happiness may seem to be as inscrutable as the will of God.

II. JEREMY BENTHAM

Within the vast, and still not completely published, body of Bentham's writings the strictly ethical element bulks very small. In effect this element consists of the first five chapters of his *Introduction to the Principles of Morals and Legislation* (1789). This book, which had been printed but not published, in a manner highly characteristic of Bentham's literary enterprises, in 1780, was the somewhat overgrown outcome of what had originally been intended as the introduction to a plan for a rational penal code. That intention was representative of Bentham's concern with the practical and minutely detailed work of carrying out a thorough reform, rationalisation and codification of the legal system, its laws, its procedure, its institutional arrangements and its system of punishments. This may explain an air of bluff impatience, an animated desire to get on with it, that surrounds Bentham's exposition and defence of his fundamental criterion against abstractly philosophical criticism. Indications that his primary interest was in the use of his principle to devise new schemes of legislation abound in the ethical part of the book. Indeed, as will be seen, his conviction of the obvious correctness of the principle of utility is too absolute to allow him to examine alternatives to it in more than a dismissive and perfunctory way.

He compares the ethical investigations of the *Principles* to pure mathematics, conceived in a very pragmatic spirit. 'One good at least', he writes in the preface, 'may result from the present publication; viz. that the more he [the author] has trespassed on the patience of the reader on this occasion, the less need he will have to do so on future ones: so that this may do to those, the office which is done, by books of pure mathematics, to books of mixed mathematics and natural philosophy.'[23] The future occasions he has in mind are enumerated on the next page:

no less than ten volumes setting forth articulated schemes of legislation of various kinds.

As we have seen, he begins with the misleadingly compact observation that pleasure and pain determine both what we shall do and what we ought to do. This formula obscures the fact that pleasure and pain must be conceived in one way in connection with what we in fact do and in another in connection with what we should do. But Bentham himself is fully aware of the difference between the agent's own happiness and the happiness of the community. 'The greatest happiness of all those whose interest is in question', he says, is 'the right and proper, and the only right and proper and universally desirable, end of human action.'[24] Utility is the production of benefit, advantage, pleasure, good or happiness; he sees no need to differentiate between the items in this list. The community whose happiness is the right and proper end of human action is a fictitious body and its interest is simply the sum of the interests of the individual men who compose it. As has been mentioned, an important issue is obscured by his failure to see the significance of the distinction between actions that conform to the principle of utility as being those that ought to be done and those of which it is at any rate not true that they ought not to be done. But towards the end of the book he draws a distinction between the spheres of law and 'private ethics' which throws some light on the question.[25] The principle of utility enjoins *probity*, which is 'forbearing to diminish' the happiness of others, and *beneficence*, which is 'studying to increase it'. Law and private ethics have the same ends, the general happiness. But not everything which is required by ethics should be made an object of legislation. Men should not be required by law to do those things they morally should do which it would be mistaken to punish them for failing to do. An offence is 'unmeet' for punishment where punishment would be groundless (because no mischief has been done), inefficacious (because it cannot prevent mischief of that kind), unprofitable (because the advantage to be gained by inflicting it is outweighed by its intrinsic evil) or needless (because the mischief can be prevented in some other and less painful way, by 'instruction', for example). Private ethics will not, of course, condemn acts for which punishment would be groundless, but it will operate where legal sanctions would be inefficacious, unprofitable or needless. Now Bentham believes that there is a rough coincidence between the sphere of probity, as he defines it, and the domain where punishment is appropriate. 'As to the rules of beneficence, these, as far as concerns matters of detail, must necessarily be abandoned in great measure to the jurisdiction of private ethics.'[26] In other words the law should be largely restricted to the prevention of harmful acts; the positive augmentation of happiness is a matter for private morality. But this coincidence between the proper sphere of law and the prevention of mischief is only approximate. 'In cases where the person is in danger, why should it not be made the duty' (Bentham means here the legal duty) 'of every man to save another from mischief, when it can be done without prejudicing himself, as well as to abstain from bringing it on him?' ('A woman's head-dress catches fire: water is at hand: a man instead of assisting to quench the fire, looks on, and laughs at it. . . . Who is there that . . . would think punishment misapplied?')[27] What all this implies is that for Bentham any opportunity to augment the general happiness presents a positive duty, and not just a possible action it would be wrong not to do.

Like Mill, Bentham maintains that a proof of the principle of utility is neither necessary nor possible. 'That which is used to prove everything else, cannot itself be proved.'[28] But it can be provided with indirect support in various ways. All men, on most occasions of their life, defer to it 'if not for the ordering of their own actions, yet for the trying of their own actions, as well as of those of other men'.[29] The trouble is that they do not follow it consistently. Bentham's main point is that 'when a man attempts to combat the principle of utility, it is with reasons drawn, without his being aware of it, from that very principle itself'.[30] There is, of course, something in this. If someone insists on reasons being provided for specific moral principles, such as those which enjoin the keeping of promises or telling the truth, there seems to

29

be nothing left to appeal to but considerations of the general good. But the traditional opponents of utilitarianism, intuitionists or deontologists like Kant and Prichard, in holding principles like these to be self-evident are committed to the view that it is a mistake to ask for reasons for them. To suppose that reasons for them must be available is, on this view, to misunderstand their nature as *moral* principles and has the effect of transforming them into counsels of prudence, individual or collective. Such theorists agree with Bentham that nothing can be proved unless something is accepted without proof; they differ from him as to what these unprovables are. They can argue, with some plausibility, that the principles they take to be ultimate are regarded as more certain and authoritative by the 'common moral consciousness'.

Bentham's view is that opposition to the principle of utility is either the outcome of sinister interest or else confusion and prejudice. The task of its defender is to expose the former and dissipate the latter. Let anyone who doubts the principle of utility, Bentham says, ask himself if he would really wish to discard it altogether. Does he propose any other principle in its place: if so, is it really a distinct principle or is it just a policy of giving a respectable form to his private and capricious sentiments? If he takes his own emotions of approval to be the criterion of morality 'let him ask himself whether his sentiment is to be a standard of right and wrong, with respect to every other man, or whether every man's sentiment has the same privilege of being a standard to itself?'[31] In the former case he is setting himself up as a moral despot; in the latter he is endorsing moral anarchy.

This general programme of refutation is put into effect in the second chapter of the *Principles*, where Bentham considers 'principles adverse to that of utility'. In this rather knockabout discussion all alternative ethical theories are subsumed under two heads. First there is the principle of asceticism, a fairly satirical version of Christian morality, which is taken to enjoin the exact opposite of the end proposed by utilitarianism, favouring the diminution and disapproving the augmentation of happiness. It has a stronger, religious form in which, inspired by the fear of God, its adherents make the pursuit of pain a duty, and a weaker, philosophical form, in which, for the sake of reputation, the grosser pleasures are rejected and the other pleasures are called by any other name than 'pleasure'. The principle of asceticism has never been applied in the public business of legislation and cannot be consistently pursued. (Bentham says the attempt to pursue it would produce a hell on earth but his underlying and less question-begging reason for denying its possibility must be its manifest conflict with the basic motivation of human conduct.) It is the outcome, to the extent that it is rational at all, of a self-destructive extrapolation of the discovery that certain immediate pleasures turn out in the long run to produce a more than equivalent amount of pain.

Secondly, there is the principle of sympathy and antipathy, or principle of caprice, which takes the mere fact of approval or disapproval as the measure of right or wrong. Into this capacious container are swept the whole variety of more or less intuitionistic ethical theories: those that base morality on a moral sense, or common sense, or a moral understanding of the fitness of things, or the law of nature, and several others. In regarding all these as equivalent to each other and as amounting to no more than a mischievous disguise for unreasoned moral prejudice Bentham greatly simplifies his task of refutation at the cost of failing to address himself to the more serious alternatives to his own position. Even the kind of subjectivism that he does indentify as the common core of these alternatives is not very convincingly disposed of. His objections to it are mostly simple moral objections that presuppose the utilitarian principle he is supposed to be defending. The principle of caprice is despotic. Although, more often than not, the results of applying it coincide with those of the principle of utility it tends to err on the side of severity. Finally Bentham adverts to the theological principle that morally right action is that which accords with the will of God. This, he maintains, is not really a new and distinct principle. What God wills must always be a matter of presumption and is always in need of interpretation. In effect the view that God's will is the criterion of morality must be reducible to one of the three principles already considered: asceticism, caprice or utility.

The real objection that lies behind what Bentham has to say about the principle of caprice is that it fails to distinguish between what men as a matter of fact approve of and what they should, if rational, approve of. Most people at least pay lip-service to the existence of such a distinction; they believe that their unreflective approvals and disapprovals are susceptible of criticism and, perhaps, amendment, if only by being adjusted to a more correct conception of the actual facts of the case in hand. But Bentham's actual procedure is not well calculated to make this point. He insists that there is a difference between the motive of an action and the ground of approval for it. We unconsciously transfer, he suggests, our approval of the effects of a moral sentiment to that sentiment itself. But a moral sentiment, such as antipathy, can never be a right ground of action; only utility can be that. Moral sentiment 'requires always to be regulated, to prevent its doing mischief. . . . The principle of utility neither requires nor admits of any other regulator than itself.'[32]

From this point on in the *Principles* Bentham's lust for classification is given its head. Following Gay, he enumerates four sanctions, or sources of pleasure and pain, capable of influencing men's conduct. There is the physical sanction of pleasant or painful natural consequences of action which occur independently of the operation of any human will. There is the political sanction, which consists principally of punishment meted out by a judge, under a sovereign. There is the popular sanction, by which 'chance persons' influence the conduct of others through various 'mortifications and inconveniences'. And, finally, there is the religious sanction, the allocation of pleasures and pains, in this life or the next, by a 'superior being'. Bentham's ostensible reasons for neglecting the religious sanction in what follows is that it is difficult to tell which advantages and misfortunes in this life do display the hand of God and even more difficult to determine what will happen in the next.

In the fourth chapter Bentham presents, very briefly, what has come to be called his hedonic calculus. Here a sevenfold distinction is employed. In order to measure the magnitude of a pleasure or pain, or to compare one pleasure or pain with another, we need to consider, first, certain properties that the pleasure or pain has considered on its own. These are its *intensity*, its *duration*, its *certainty* of actually taking place and its *propinquity*, its distance in time from the calculation. It has often been pointed out that, if the certainty of a future pleasure or pain is allowed for, its propinquity is irrelevant. Remoteness in time is fairly generally associated with uncertainty but it does not make any difference except as a reason for uncertainty. Secondly, there are two causal relationships in which pleasures and pains stand to other pleasures and pains: *fecundity*, 'the chance it has of being followed by sensations of the same kind' and *purity*, 'the chance it has of not being followed by sensations of the opposite kind.[33] Finally, in all cases where the interests of a number of people are in question, the *extent*, or number of people affected, needs to be taken into consideration.

These seven properties are described by Bentham as the *dimensions* of pleasure and pain and he says that in estimating the tendency of an action we must first take an account of the value of each pleasure and pain that it will produce, directly or indirectly, and then balance the sum of pleasures against the sum of pains. Arithmetical terminology abounds in his discussion. But it is not at all clear that it is meant to be taken with absolute literalness. The obvious objection to Bentham's use of the word 'dimension' for the various ways in which pleasures can be assessed is that it implies a comparison with measurement of volume in the three dimensions of space. But in the latter case there are units of measurement that are just the same when applied to height or depth or width: there are measuring-rods which can be aligned with what is to be measured in all dimensions. There is no such congruity between the items in Bentham's list, no common unit correlating a certain amount of intensity with a certain amount of duration. At most we can say that a comparison of pleasures which takes all of Bentham's dimensions into account is better, more rational, than one that does not. The use of the 'calculus' is to remind us of what we must take into consideration if our assessment of two alternative possibilities is to be complete. Bentham does say that such calculations should not be undertaken in the case of each particular act, and even, more surprisingly, in the case of every 'legislative operation'. The procedure should, however, be 'kept in view'. There are, of course, good utilitarian reasons for this economy of calculation; in particular, we often need to act quickly if any utility is to be realised at all.

In most of the rest of the *Principles* Bentham luxuriates in classificatory self-indulgence. One variety of simple pleasure, the pleasure of sense, has itself nine forms. Pleasure and pain are not directly proportional to the external factors that excite them. Human sensibility varies, for no less than thirty-two different kinds of reason. This taxonomical orgy is followed by a long discussion of the nature and mental causes of the antecedents of action: the intention behind it, the consciousness or beliefs that accompany it, its underlying motive and the disposition to which the presence of that motive testifies. The point of this discussion is to assemble the material for a rational theory of punishment. For, he says, 'the business of government is to promote the happiness of the society, by punishing and rewarding,'[34] a somewhat reductive point of view.

Only in the final chapter, on the limits of the penal branch of jurisprudence, does he return to anything of general ethical interest: the distinction between law and private ethics discussed earlier, and his somewhat parenthetical solution to the problem of moral motivation. 'What motives', he asks, '(independent of such as religion and legislation may chance to furnish) can one man have to consult the happiness of another?'[35] His reply is that on all occasions there is the social motive of sympathy and benevolence, and, in addition, there are the 'semi-social' motives of love and amity and reputation, a thesis further developed in J. S. Mill's account of the internal sanctions of morality.

Bentham's *Principles* is something of a mechanical contraption for much of its considerable length. But it would be wrong to leave it without giving an example of Bentham's lively and generous humanitarianism. This footnote on fanaticism shows that Bentham was no impersonal and desiccated moral calculator. 'If a man happens to take it into his head to assassinate with his own hands, or with the sword of justice, those whom he calls heretics, that is, people who think, or perhaps only speak, differently upon a subject which neither party understands, he will be as much inclined to do this at one time as at another. Fanaticism never sleeps: it is never glutted: it is never stopped by philanthropy; for it makes a merit of trampling on philanthropy: it is never stopped by conscience; for it has pressed conscience into its service. Avarice, lust and vengeance, have piety, benevolence and honour; fanaticism has nothing to oppose it.'[36]

There is no need to spend much time on James Mill. His ethical writings were the least significant of his many services to utilitarianism in general and to Bentham in particular. His main theoretical achievement was the systematic presentation of the associationist theory of the development of the mind, which the utilitarians derived, by way of Hartley and Priestley, from Hume, in his large *Analysis of the Phenomena of the Human Mind*. The chief relevance to ethics of this theory is the account it contains of the way in which the moral sentiment of benevolence, a steady regard for the general happiness, is derived from the initially self-regarding impulses of man. Mill insists that the fact that the social or other-regarding sentiments can be causally explained in self-regarding terms does not mean that they do not really exist. Mill's psychology provided utilitarianism with a theory of education, a thoroughly environmentalist one, on the same lines as that of Helvétius. It was put into fairly terrifying practice, as we learn from the *Autobiography* of John Stuart Mill. Perhaps James Mill's most significant influence was exercised through the political theory, presented in his *Essay on Government*, which converted Bentham to democracy from his earlier confidence in the enlightened despotism of a truly rational and philanthropic legislator, the *deus ex machina*, who, mysteriously exempt from ordinary human frailties, is to bring about an artificial harmony of interests by the introduction of a brand-new system of laws. Mill's point is very simple. The end of government is the general happiness; the only group of people who can be guaranteed to have a reliable interest in the pursuit of this end is the public at large. Democracy, by making the rulers' continuance in power dependent on their being seen to pursue the general happiness, provides them with an adequate self-regarding motive for legislating and governing in the way they should. Mill mitigated the democratic implications of this theory by maintaining that it is quite sufficient to restrict the vote to the fathers of families who, by reason of the ties of natural affection, can be counted on to represent the interests of their womenfolk and sons under forty.

James Mill's main purely ethical work is his last, the quaintly named *Fragment on Mackintosh* (1835). The strictly ethical interest of this substantial volume is almost negligible. For the most part it consists of the type of ponderous abuse that is often employed for the relief of self-righteous indignation. The abuse was not undeserved. Mackintosh's critique of utilitarianism was fatuous and superficial. Mill was right to take exception to the view that Bentham and his disciples 'clung to their opinions because they were obnoxious' or that they were concerned to wrong 'the most respectable feelings of mankind.' But Mill's controversial manner, with its futile hair-splitting and theatrical apostrophes, undermines the case he wants to make. By any standards, the utilitarian included, the *Fragment* is an immoral volume. Mill was perhaps unfortunate in having such a very flimsy antagonist to refute.

There are a few points of interest. Against moral sense theories Mill argues that utilitarianism is more economical: no special faculty is needed to explain the perception of utility. Mackintosh had argued that by allowing exceptions to the established specific principles of morality utilitarianism was an encouragement to laxity. Mill strenuously retorts that the only exceptions allowed by utilitarians are those sanctioned by utility itself, by the general interest and not, as Mackintosh had implied, by private interest. A large issue is raised here but not very deeply explored.

Mackintosh holds that there are some, intrinsically base, things, which a truly moral man would never do, however they contributed to public utility. Mill replies, in effect, that this is frivolous if the public utility is really at stake. Bentham had committed himself to the view that the motives of action, being desires for what is itself good, are themselves always good. The morality of an action depends on its intention, defined as the whole of the expected consequences of the action. Mill loyally supports this account of motives and intentions. Like Bentham he makes no clear distinction between the *rightness* of an action, to be determined by its consequences, expected or expectable, and its *praiseworthiness* or virtue, a property of the agent rather than the deed, to be determined by the motive which led him to do what he did. Mill does suggest that the consequences that 'might have been foreseen' are more relevant than those that were actually expected, but does not develop the point. Like all hedonists Mill is compelled to protest that utilitarians are not, as Mackintosh alleges, indifferent to the 'pleasures of taste and imagination' and interested only in 'visible and tangible' pleasures. Finally, Mill takes a clear position about the logical status of the principle of utility. 'The theory of utility', he says, 'makes the utility of an act and the morality of an act two names for the same thing.' In other words for him the principle of utility is an analytic truth, true in virtue of the meanings of the words of which it is composed. But this is a somewhat parenthetical observation and Mill does not explore its implications. In particular, he does not ask how those who have denied it could have failed to be aware that they were guilty of self-contradiction.

III. JOHN STUART MILL

(i) INTRODUCTORY

James Mill's education of his son was in strict conformity with the recommendations of Helvétius. The instilling of Bentham's unqualified version of the greatest happiness principle was a central ingredient in it. That principle was used by Bentham in a radically critical way to undermine conventional assumptions. John Stuart Mill came to turn the kind of rationalism it exemplified against the principle itself.

We know, from his *Autobiography* and from the essays on Bentham and Coleridge which he wrote in his early thirties and published soon after the deaths of Bentham and his father, that Mill was deeply dissatisfied with the conception of human nature embodied in the teaching to which they had subjected him. In his early twenties he had lapsed into a state of emotional prostration as a result of his father's educational regime. He says that Wordsworth's poetry played a large part in his spiritual recovery. In the related ideas of Coleridge he found an intellectual equivalent, an altogether more perceptive account of human needs and powers than the one that he had been brought up to believe in.

Thus in *Utilitarianism*, published in 1863 when Mill was in his middle fifties, there are several heretical deviations from Benthamite orthodoxy. The most conspicuous of these is his distinction between higher and lower qualities of pleasure. Another is his emphasis on conscience as derived from the social instincts of man in contrast to the Hobbesian account of the essentially self-interested nature of human motivation given by Bentham and his father. The book begins with a survey of criticisms of utilitarian ethics which tends to meet them half way as much as to rebut them. As a result of these modifications Mill's utilitarianism is very much his own.

In his other writings in relevant fields, in particular on politics, he departs even further from the letter of his intellectual inheritance. *On Liberty*, for example, is only vestigially utilitarian. The ultimate value on which his defence of freedom, personal, intellectual and political, depends is the self-development and perfection of the individual. He relates this to the utilitarian end of the general happiness only in passing, by way of a reference to 'the permanent interests of man as a progressive being',[37] a more flexible and elusive notion than happiness as Bentham conceived it.

All the same, in spite of the insecure and marginal character of his commitment to it, Mill's essay has always been and is likely to remain the authoritative exposition of utilitarian ethics. There are several reasons for this. In the first place his book is short, lucid and eloquent. Secondly it is exclusively concerned with utilitarian *ethics*, a topic which Bentham hurried past on his way to the more engrossing subject of public legislation. Finally it is more philosophically satisfying than Bentham's breezy dogmatism. Mill offers his famous 'proof' of the principle of utility and develops its consequences with sensitive attention to difficulties that Bentham would have brushed aside. Mill admirably combines candour with perceptiveness.

(ii) THE REMOVAL OF MISUNDERSTANDINGS

The second chapter of the book, 'What Utilitarianism Is', after setting out Mill's well-known definition of 'the creed which accepts as the foundation of morals, Utility or the Greatest Happiness Principle', is mainly concerned to remove misunderstandings. Three at least of these are verbal, turning on the words *utility*, *expediency* and *pleasure*. To regard utility as the foundation of morals is not, he points out, to deny the value of pleasure, but is emphatically to affirm it. To possess utility is to be valuable derivatively, by reason of consequences that are valuable in themselves and the only intrinsic, or non-consequential, value is pleasure and the absence of pain. Again when utilitarians ascribe the rightness of actions to their expediency they are not using this word in the colloquial sense in which it is contrasted with principle. The expediency they have in mind is general or public expediency which, in their view, is what principle in fact amounts to, as opposed to the private expediency of self-interest.

These are minor points that need only to be made in order to forestall the tactics of unscrupulous debaters. The interpretation of pleasure as it figures in the utilitarian principle is a more serious matter. Mill was very sensitive to the accusation that utilitarianism was a pig-philosophy, a Cyrenaic endorsement of voluptuousness. It is hard to doubt that Bentham's emphasis on the word, and his connected view that happiness is no more than a sum or aggregation of pleasures, was deliberately provocative. Mill, at any rate, found it an embarrassing inheritance.

It is clear that the first thing that the word *pleasure* puts us in mind of is what may be called bodily or animal pleasures, what Mill was to call the lower pleasures, whose full achievement would still leave Socrates dissatisfied. It is with this application that the word appears in such phrases as 'the pursuit of pleasure' or 'man of pleasure' or 'pleasure-lover'. As the word is ordinarily employed these phrases serve to distinguish some lines of conduct and some types of human being from others. But in Bentham's extended sense they must apply to all intended acts and to all men.

The elementary pleasures of eating, drinking, sexuality, resting and so forth have a number of properties that are broadly common and peculiar to them. First of all, they essentially involve bodily sensation. Secondly, they are almost universally enjoyed, at least to the extent that failure to enjoy them is ordinarily conceived as a basic constitutional abnormality and as in need of explanation. A third feature, connected with their universality, is the fact that they can be profoundly enjoyable although no effort has been involved in experiencing them, in particular that of training for them or acquiring a taste for them. Of course effort is usually necessary to secure the external means to these satisfactions, the meals, drinks or sexual partners required for them. If not too laborious these efforts may augment the satisfactions that reward them. But the satisfaction is not much diminished if it is achieved without effort. Again training in cookery, the choice of wine and amatory technique may intensify the pleasures with which they are connected but they are only indispensable in special and unusual circumstances of jadedness through indulgence.

Finally it is characteristic of pleasures in the colloquial, bodily sense to be much more intensely gratifying than more elevated or spiritual satisfactions. The pains of deprivation are also correspondingly more intense in these cases. But this intensity is very closely linked to short duration. Bodily pleasures tend to preoccupy the consciousness of those who enjoy them while they last but they do not last for very long. This defect of fleetingness does not seem to be compensated for by a correspondingly limited endurance of the pains of being deprived of these sources of pleasure. Hunger, thirst and, perhaps to a lesser extent, sexual frustration show considerable staying power.

Elementary animal pleasures, then, are bodily, universal, need neither effort nor skill for their enjoyment and are characteristically intense although short-lived. If they are what is first brought to mind by the word *pleasure* they do not wholly appropriate it in its colloquial use. Stamp-collecting, deep-sea fishing and playing the cello can be described as pleasures without any trace of metaphor or figurativeness, and so can professional achievement, friendship or being the parent of happy, healthy and successful children. Recreations involve specific bodily activities but of a kind which are negligibly gratifying in themselves; achievements have no definite bodily aspect. Recreations are far from universally pleasing although most achievements, if conceived in a fairly generic way, would seem to be. Both require effort and skill. The pleasure of a recreation cannot be enjoyed at all unless it is engaged in for a period much longer than the ordinary duration of a direct bodily delight. The pleasure of an achievement is necessarily protracted; it is a continuously satisfying background to the detailed activities and incidents of life.

The cluster of rather significant structural properties that are characteristic of the elementary pleasures provides a good reason for distinguishing among the extremely heterogeneous array of things to which the word *pleasure* can be properly applied or, as Mill puts it, for distinguishing qualities of pleasure. What is questionable about Mill's position on this topic is that he takes this distinction of quality in an evaluative way. To dispel the accusation that the utilitarian advocates the supreme value of bodily gratification he seems to say that a non-bodily pleasure is more valuable than a bodily pleasure that is its quantitative equal, or even superior, in pleasantness. This, at any rate, is what he has been generally taken to mean and with good cause.

To start with, he explicitly says, 'it would be absurd that ... the estimation of pleasures should be supposed to depend on quantity alone'.[38] Secondly, he plainly rejects the argument a strict Benthamite would employ to demonstrate the superiority of mental to bodily pleasure from what he calls the 'circumstantial advantages' of the former: its greater 'permanency, safety, uncostliness'. The strict Benthamite, or consistent hedonist, would argue that the commonly high estimation, at least in practice, of the pleasures of the body is due to a misguided obsession with intensity at the expense of the other 'dimensions' in which quantitative differences between pleasures are to be found, according to the doctrine of the hedonic calculus. The pleasures of friendship or cello-playing are no doubt less intense than those of heavy eating or dedicated sexuality but they are more enduring, in that they can be practised for a much longer time before pleasure turns into its opposite, are more fecund, in that they can be more pleasurably repeated, and more pure, in that there is less likelihood with them of associated displeasure. Mill does not deny the validity of this line of reasoning as far as it goes but its adherents, he says, 'might have taken the other, and, as it may be called, higher ground, with entire consistency'.

But, as Mill's critics have generally agreed, such a view is *not* consistent with the hedonistic principle that pleasure alone is valuable in itself. If two situations are identical with regard to the amount of pleasure they contain, and, one should add, give rise to, then, if they differ in value, it must be on account of something other than pleasure. Mill's confusion on this point may have been assisted by the fact that *quality*, most notably in the language of advertisement, is itself often an evaluative word.

What has not been noticed is that the reason Mill gives for supposing that mental pleasures are more valuable than bodily ones can very naturally be interpreted as reinstating the identification of value with quantity of pleasure that he ostensibly rejects. His argument for the superiority is that of those who have had a wide experience of pleasures of both kinds all, or almost all, give a 'decided preference' to the former. But what can this decided preference be but the outward sign of a stronger desire for the kind of pleasure preferred? Mill's view is that to desire something is to think it pleasant. It would seem to follow that to desire one thing more than another is to think that it is the more pleasant of the two, to estimate it as quantitatively the greater pleasure.

It is a reasonable conclusion that the intensely respectable Mill was thrown off balance by the kind of moral objection to utilitarianism that Bentham's provocative emphasis on the word 'pleasure' invites. If pleasures are to be compared at all as greater and less it is irrational to concentrate on their intensity to the exclusion of all other respects in which they may relevantly differ. In fact, despite his lip-service to the validity of the circumstantial argument for the superiority of mental to bodily pleasures, Mill does not believe in the hedonic calculus with which it is associated. He insists that pleasures and pains are far too heterogeneous for any mechanical routine of computation to yield acceptable estimations of their quantity of the sort Bentham had in mind. But to deny that pleasure and pain can be appraised by a numerical calculus is not to deny that they can be compared in a more total and impressionistic way and any such comparison will be rational just to the extent that it takes relevant factors other than intensity into account.

None of the other objections that Mill considers in this chapter lead to such substantial amendments of the utilitarianism he derived from Bentham. Two of them are fairly trivial; three others are important in principle but in the form in which Mill confronts them their real point is not made. The two trivial objections are that utilitarianism is godless and that it 'renders men cold and unsympathetic' by fixing their attention on the consequences of actions rather than on the characters of their agents. The example of Paley was available to show that as long as God moves in an unmysterious way, as long as his benevolence consists in a desire for his creatures' happiness in a sense that they can recognise and understand, God's commands can be shown to coincide with the dictates of the principles of utility. On the other point Mill reasonably observes that utilitarian ethics is, in the first instance, a theory of the rightness of actions. Such a theory does not exclude a theory of the praiseworthiness of agents. If it should be completed with an account of virtue or moral goodness this need not differ in form from that with which any theory of right action, however unutilitarian, might be associated, namely that a morally good or virtuous agent is one whose dispositions are calculated to lead to right actions. Since, for utilitarianism, right action leads to general happiness it would seem that benevolence, a desire for the happiness of all, would be the supreme virtue, in his view. It is certainly hard for the utilitarian to detach benevolence from conscientiousness, the desire to act rightly, in the manner of sterner moralities like those of Butler and Kant. To desire the means, right conduct, is to desire its necessary and defining end, the general happiness.

The three more serious objections whose potential force, I have said, Mill does not appreciate, are that happiness is unattainable, that utilitarianism demands too much of men in the way of public spirit and self-effacement, and that it imposes requirements of calculation on moral agents which it is impossible to satisfy.

Mill is disposed to regard the objection that happiness is unattainable as largely a verbal quibble but with a significant point underlying it: that in an imperfect world some self-sacrifice must be required from us. It may well be true that men cannot be absolutely happy all the time, but they can still obtain some happiness. There is a certain lack of polemical energy about this reply. Two powerful considerations that he could have appealed to are, first, that the utilitarian end is not the achievement of total and unqualified happiness but its maximisation to the greatest possible extent together with the greatest possible minimisation of pain and, secondly, that an ideal of conduct does not have to be strictly attainable to be effective: doctors are right not to yield to any discouragement arising from the knowledge that all men are mortal.

The more serious point underlying the objection is that the Benthamite definition of happiness as a sum of pleasures is far too neat and simple to be adequate. Mill does not explicitly dissent from the orthodox formula but he comes near to undermining it when he says that for happiness men need both tranquillity, in which absence of pain is secured at the cost of a low level of pleasure, and excitement, in which intense pleasure is likely but with the added risk of much pain. However, utilitarianism can easily survive the rejection of Bentham's over-simplified additive reduction of happiness to pleasure. The inadequacy of this reduction does not mean that happiness has to be conceived as some mysterious and unanalysable state, logically unrelated to pleasure. A man is happy to the extent that his more persistent and deep-seated desires are either satisfied or are known by him to be readily satisfiable. No aggregation of intense bodily delights can compensate for the frustration of long-term and serious desires for more than a short time. Nevertheless pleasure, in the inclusive sense of the word, remains the essential ingredient of happiness.[39]

A more sophisticated version of this criticism is advanced in the chapter on 'pleasure for pleasure's sake' in Bradley's *Ethical Studies*. Bradley argues that since pleasure is something passing and evanescent, a 'perishing series' is the quaint phrase he uses for it, it is not a logically acceptable general end of conduct. I shall return to this later when I come to consider three classical criticisms of utilitarian ethics.

Mill's observation that self-sacrifice is morally inevitable in an imperfect world is introduced as an acceptable practical limitation to the complete achievement of the utilitarian end. The real difficulty this fact presents is not to his conception of the moral end. (That end is the *general* happiness and it is not surprising that it should require some foregoing of possible individual happiness.) What it does conflict with is the egoistic theory of motivation associated with utilitarian ethics. Mill's solution to that problem is, in the end, Hobbesian. Self-sacrifice is, he argues, despite appearances, a way of satisfying one's desires. By enabling us to rise above fate it contributes to happiness.

The second major objection he considers is that utilitarianism makes too heavy a demand on the moral virtue of the individual. Mill's initial answer, that an action can be right whatever the motive from which it is undertaken, does not really meet it. For the theory does entail that in every situation of choice the agent *ought* to choose that of the options available to him which will make the largest contribution to the general happiness. Mill's initial answer is that in many cases agents will straightforwardly want to choose the most publicly beneficial course anyway. Now this seems reasonable enough if the principle involved is not taken too strictly. It is very often true that agents in a situation of choice do not unreflectively want to do something that will significantly *detract* from the general happiness. Some such negative interpretation of the fundamental utilitarian principle of conduct seems to lie behind Mill's observation that most ordinary people are very seldom in a position to make any significant positive contribution to the general welfare, although they can often act so as to diminish it. But, unless an unplausibly fatalistic conception of what people could do for the general happiness is embraced, this objection can be met only by recasting the principle of utility, as a thesis about morals, in a negative way. In most situations of life people are not doing any positive harm but it is also true that they could be doing more positive good than they are doing, even when this good is not merely that of others but is taken to include their own happiness.

The essential point is that the principle of utility divides all possible choices into two classes: that of what definitely ought to be done, which in every situation, except those in which two or more choices are both equally beneficial and more beneficial than any other alternative, will be unique, and that of what definitely ought not to be done. Thus every choice that is not morally compulsory is morally forbidden. The only morally indifferent choices the principle can countenance are those between alternatives that are at once equally and supremely beneficial.

Even a negative formulation of the principle of utility will not avoid this kind of moral totalitarianism if it requires action to minimise suffering. In most ordinary situations of morally acceptable conduct there is probably something more that the agent could have done to achieve this end than he did. What is needed is a *limited* negative formulation of the principle which lays down that every action that reduces the general happiness should be avoided, unless every possible alternative would reduce it still more. Mill's remarks about the capacity of ordinary agents to augment or diminish the general happiness have the effect of so circumscribing that capacity that the usual unrestricted principle amounts to no more in practical application than its limited, negative version. But the limits he sets to human moral capacity are unrealistically narrow. It may be that men cannot be reasonably expected or enjoined to act in a very much more public-spirited way than they usually do but it seems clear that they could do so all the same.

The third and last of these more serious objections is that utilitarian ethics lays an impossible burden of calculation on the moral agent. In every situation it requires him to determine all the possible lines of action he could adopt, including inaction, and then to calculate what the total consequences for the general happiness of each of these alternatives would be. Mill presents the difficulty in concretely practical terms, as arising from the time the required deliberation would take. His indirect, and rhetorically expressed, answer is that the time available is that of the elapsed and recorded moral experience of the human race. That accumulated experience provides us with knowledge of the moral *tendency* of actions of particular kinds, embodied in rules or principles that are subordinate to the principle of utility itself.

This is one of two clear pieces of evidence that Mill was a rule-utilitarian and not an act-utilitarian. In other words his position was not that an act is right because it has good consequences but because it is an act of a kind which generally has good consequences. The other place where he appears to subscribe to the rule-utilitarian doctrine is in his main formulation of the principle of utility, where he says that an act is right if it *tends* to promote happiness. An individual action cannot have a tendency. Producing certain effects more often than not cannot be a characteristic of an individual action which occurs once and once only and has one and only one set of effects. Only a kind or class of actions can have a tendency to promote happiness or anything else.

The necessity of rules, or subordinate principles, as yielding economies of calculation, has been argued for on utilitarian grounds. Effective, value-realising action very often needs to be swift; opportunities pass. Furthermore time should not be wasted. The more of it that is taken up in deliberation the less there will be for effective action. Any greater refinement in evaluation that might be secured by carefully thinking out alternative possible outcomes in a situation of choice is very unlikely to outweigh the benefits of rapidity conferred by reliance on rules. This argument applies the principle of the division of labour to the domain of moral activity. It holds that the reflective task of elaborating general rules of beneficial conduct should be undertaken on the one hand *by* specially qualified people, that is to say moralists, or, on the other, *during* periods of time that are free from exigencies of action. In this way a stock of ready-made rules will be made available for moral agents confronted with the need for choice.

I do not think that this style of argument for rule-utilitarianism gets to the root of the matter. I believe it can be shown that something like rule-utilitarianism must be accepted by any theory which evaluates actions in the light of their consequences. One argument for this conclusion turns on the reasonable, but disputable, view that the consequences of an action that are relevant to its moral quality are not those which it actually has but those which it would be reasonable for an agent to expect it to have.

Another, perhaps more securely based, is derived from the widely held assumption that regularity is an essential element in the concept of causality which must be used in the calculation of consequences.

The first of these arguments may be introduced by reference to a threefold distinction drawn by C. I. Lewis.[40] An action, he says, is *absolutely* right if it has the best actual consequences, *objectively* right if it is reasonable to expect that it will have the best consequences and *subjectively* right if its agent expects it to have the best consequences. Which of these is the central concept? Clearly not that of subjective rightness, for we should naturally say of someone who did an act that was subjectively but not objectively right that he thought that what he was doing was right but that in fact it was not. A reason for taking the objective concept rather than the absolute one as central is that the person to whom the notion of rightness is of primary importance is the agent, who has to decide about its application before the possible action to which it is applied has actually taken place, and therefore before any of its consequences have come about. Only the subsequent critic of action is in a position to determine what is absolutely right. The most the agent can know and act on is the objective rightness of actions. An objectively right act could be described as right *simpliciter* and one which is absolutely but not objectively right, which has unpredictably good consequences, as a merely fortunate act.

If we make this assumption, that a right act is one which it is rational to expect will have the best consequences, something like rule-utilitarianism inevitably follows. For the possible act that is judged right can be expected to have good consequences only by way of the generally beneficial tendency of the set of properties by which it is defined. It is possible for me to do A or B. A is right as against B since its rationally expectable consequences X are better than B's rationally expectable consequences Y. But for A to have the consequences X is only a rational expectation if it is generally the case that acts of *kind* A have consequences of *kind* X. The reasoning required for a rational

49

expectation that a particular act of kind A will have good consequences is inevitably sufficient to establish the rule that acts of kind A are right or, in a comparative case of the sort I started from, that an act of kind A is right as against an act of kind B.

It is now easy to see that it is not essential to the argument that the rightness of an action should be defined in terms of its rationally expectable consequences. Suppose, instead, that rightness is taken in what Lewis calls its absolute sense. In that case the most authoritative and least conjectural judgement about the rightness of an action will have to be made after the event. Now one form such a judgement could take is comparative. We have to compare the consequences of the action actually performed with those of the possible alternatives to it. But, since these, *ex hypothesi*, have not been performed, all that can be done is to work out what consequences *it* would be rational to expect that they would have had if they had been performed, that is what the general tendency is of actions of those possible, but in this case unperformed, kinds.

If the judgement is comparative, then, at least the consequences of the unperformed alternatives have to be worked out in general terms. But this appeal to general regularities must also be present in establishing the consequences of the act that actually was performed. This is somewhat concealed by the fact that its consequences, unlike those of its alternatives, really occur, but they still have to be selected from the broad array of states of affairs which temporally follow it, to the vast majority of which it will be causally irrelevant. Its consequences proper have to be picked out from the mass of its mere successors, and this can be done only by reference to the known general tendencies of acts of its kind. From this it also follows that, even if judgements of rightness are non-comparative, they have to be based on general truths about the kinds of actions in which the action in question is included. In other words, even if all that has to be considered in deciding whether a particular action is right is its actual consequences these still have to be discriminated, within the large class of events and states which temporally succeed it, by reference to knowledge about the kind of events and states which regularly follow actions of that kind.

This is a very abstract argument and I have been careful to claim no more for it than that it establishes 'something like rule-utilitarianism'. For in the type of case which might seem least propitious for rule-utilitarianism, a non-comparative judgement of the absolute rightness of an action that has actually been performed, although some of the materials for a rule are present the reasoning may not be throughout of the generality required for a rule to be formulated.

Action a_1 of kind A has been performed. It is temporally followed by events and states of affairs $b, c, d \ldots h, i, j \ldots p, q, r$. To pick out c, i and q as its consequences I have to rely on the causal propositions A *causes* C, C *causes* I and I *causes* Q. I also have to rely on what may be called hedonic propositions to establish the goodness of these consequences. If these are of the form C *is pleasant*, then I am in a position to say that, provided the other consequences of A are not so bad as to outweigh this, A is right. But it is possible that $c, i,$ and q, the particular consequences of a_1, are pleasant, although this is not true of $C, I,$ and Q generally. In that case the generality of the premises from which *a is right* is derived is not complete enough for the corresponding rule *A is right* to be established. So only if the hedonic quality of a particular state of affairs is regularly associated with its other properties, in particular those of its properties which would be mentioned in causal propositions about it, will the premises of a utilitarian judgement of rightness contain the materials for a rule. But it seems reasonable to suppose that these hedonic qualities are regularly associated with the other properties of the states of affairs that they characterise. For unless this were the case the pursuit of pleasure and the avoidance of pain would be a much more random and chancy affair than it is. Finally, the fact that the materials for establishing a rule are present in the reasoning that underlies a judgement of rightness does not entail that any such rule is actually formulated. It may facilitate a much greater flexibility in judging the rightness of acts to assemble causal and hedonic knowledge separately. A reason for this is that a great many different pieces of causal and hedonic knowledge may be relevant to a particular judgement of rightness which may be needed in quite different combinations on other occasions.

In the form in which Mill confronts it, the objection that utilitarianism demands too much in the way of calculation is practical. But there is a logical objection to its requirements of calculation which he does not raise. This is that the consequences of an action extend indefinitely into its future and, therefore, that an evaluation of its total consequences is logically impossible. The legendary horse-shoe nail whose loss led to that of a horse, a rider, a charge, a battle, a war and a kingdom is a favourite instance of the incompletable openness of an action's consequences.

It is a virtue of the objective conception of rightness, as Lewis defines it, that it is not exposed to this objection. What is rationally predictable at any given time, in the light of the necessarily finite body of knowledge available at that time, must itself be limited. But this advantage draws attention to a countervailingly unattractive implication of the objective concept. This is that the rightness of an action is relative to the time, more specifically to the state of knowledge prevailing at the time, at which it was decided upon. A type of conduct that was right a hundred years ago may no longer be right, now that we know that its probable consequences are not what it was then rational to expect they would be, even though there has been no change in the relevant external circumstances, in the consequences which actually follow actions of that type, and only a change in the knowledge that an agent can reasonably be expected to have of them. But perhaps the implication is not insupportably unattractive. For it does not follow that any particular action was right at the time it was performed, but subsequently became wrong. The rightness of any particular action is defined, according to the objective concept, in relation to the time it was decided upon, whatever may be the time at which its rightness is being considered.

Suppose that, shortly after his birth, Adolf Hitler was being carried by a decrepit great-aunt who slipped and was confronted with a choice between dropping the infant in a way that would inevitably prove fatal to it or suffering a heavy and painful fall herself. What should she have done? Nearly everyone would have been better off if she had made the former choice and, by dropping the baby, have prevented Nazism, the Second World War and the final solution of the Jewish problem. It would have been the absolutely right decision in Lewis's sense. Since she could not possibly have known the benefits that would accrue to mankind from making the first choice, her decision to take all the unpleasant immediate consequences of her slip on herself was plainly the objectively right thing to do. It is hardly open to doubt that this second choice, however unfortunate it turned out to be, was also the right one pure and simple.

But in fact, although the objective concept does escape the objection of indefinite consequences altogether, there is still an argument by means of which the absolute concept can avoid most of its impact. This argument draws on the plurality of causes to show that the share of the badness of some consequential state of affairs attributable to individual causal factors decreases as some multiple of their remoteness. In the Hitler example it is reasonable to suppose that his historically disastrous personality was fully formed in infancy. No doubt humiliations and disappointments in his early life contributed to it and must, therefore, share some of the causal responsibility for it. But even if his personality was innate, a vast array of contributory conditions had to obtain for it to be able to exercise its massively maleficent effect: the treaty of Versailles, the German inflation of the 1920s, Stalin's policy for the German Communist party and so on.

In general, the colloquial convenience of picking out some notably manageable or unusual factor as *the* cause of a given state of affairs should not be allowed to obscure the fact that a large number of conditions must obtain for any effect to be produced. Causes are always plural. It follows that the direct causal ancestry of an effect multiplies with each step backwards in the effect's causal hierarchy. Many of these causal progenitors of an event will either be human actions or events that human action could have prevented, and thus within the proper domain of moral judgement. Given that at each stage the plurality of causes involved is fairly numerous the proportion of responsibility for the effect that can be reasonably imputed to any single factor at any remote stage will be vanishingly small.

In the case of the lost horse-shoe the farrier cannot be given all the blame for the loss of the kingdom. The rider should have been adroit enough to survive the horse's fall; the troop commander should not have ordered a charge whose chances of success were so finely balanced; the army commander should have been able to overcome the misfortune of an unsuccessful charge; and so on. The final disaster, in other words, was the result of a collaborative effort, in which many besides the careless farrier participated.

(iii) THE SANCTIONS OF MORALITY

Having removed as misunderstandings what were offered as objections, and having, in the course of doing so, introduced his damaging and unnecessary qualification about qualities of pleasure, Mill turns to the question of explaining the motives men have for conforming their conduct to the principle of utility. It is not clear why Mill should have chosen to take up the topic of the motives of morality at this stage in his exposition. The principle of utility is the crucial element in an account of the meaning of moral judgements or, it might be less abrupt to say, an account of the rational method of arriving at moral judgements; it provides an ultimate criterion of truth for such judgements. The question which he now raises – why should anyone act on such judgements, how can their practical effect on conduct be psychologically explained – is apparently independent of the initial question of their validity.

For most of the last fifty years moral philosophers have been developing theories in which the practical, action-guiding force of moral judgements is taken to be an essential part of their meaning. An influential example of theories of this kind is that a moral

principle is, and a moral judgement implies, a universal imperative, of the form: *let everyone do X in circumstances Y*. Such a theory
gives an account of the meaning of moral affirmations which
automatically settles the question about motives. No one will
seriously call on everyone, including himself, to act in a certain
way unless he wants himself and others to act in that way. The
difficulty for theories of this kind is the subjectivisation of morality
that it implies. Agreement in moral attitudes becomes accidental,
or at least contingent. Again, while it is clear enough why one
who makes a moral judgement should guide his own actions in
accordance with it, it is not at all clear why his expression of it to
anyone else should be supposed to be effective unless they happen
to share his moral attitudes or fear him or aim to please him.

Mill's concern with motivation may be a sign that he does
implicitly recognise that practical effectiveness is somehow
intimately bound up with moral judgements. A more direct
incentive to taking up the question is provided by one of the
essential elements of his 'proof' of the principle of utility in the
chapter following that in which he discusses the sanctions of
morality. He argues there that the only thing that men desire for its
own sake is pleasure. If the assumption, which he undoubtedly
made, that all action is prompted by desire, is added to this
thesis, the conclusion follows that all action is ultimately for the
sake of the agent's own pleasure. In the light of this conclusion
Mill, if he is to represent moral judgements, in their utilitarian
interpretation, as practically effective, must show that the pursuit
of the general happiness is or can be a source of pleasure to men,
that it is an actual or rational object of desire, that it is pleasing in
itself or is a means to pleasure.

But, placed as it is before the argument that the principle of
utility depends on the hedonistic theory of motivation, Mill's
consideration of the sanctions of morality is a little confusing. It
is one thing to inquire how men are to find out what they morally
ought to do, another to ask whether they can be expected, and
how they can be got, to do it.

Bentham's account of the sanctions of morality is largely

Hobbesian and external. Our actions can be influenced by their natural consequences, occurring independently of the human will, by the state through its penal institutions, by the reactions of our fellow-humans to what we do and by the reactions of God in this life and the next. Mill begins by recognising that the principle of utility, because it is not the customary basis of morality, is not an object of unreflective moral emotion. The idea of deviation from it does not immediately excite the same disapproval as a familiar moral offence. He also recognises that there are external sanctions: 'the hope of favour and the fear of displeasure, from our fellow-creatures or from the Ruler of the Universe'.[41] But his main emphasis is on the internal sanctions: 'the conscientious feelings of mankind'.

There is a kind of natural basis for these conscientious feelings in sympathy with and affection for our fellows; but conscience itself is something more than these natural emotions. 'It is a pain, more or less intense, attendant on violation of duty, which in properly cultivated moral natures rises, in the more serious cases, into shrinking from it as an impossibility.'[42] Even if it is acquired rather than innate, as Mill's reference to 'properly cultivated moral natures' seems to suggest, it is still natural, as much as it is to speak or reason, or to live in societies, for whose secure continuance the existence of a measure of concern for the general welfare among their members is an indispensable condition. 'The moral faculty, if not a part of our nature, is a natural outgrowth from it.'[43]

Mill allows that education can cause the moral faculty to develop in any of a number of directions. He admits, too, that subsequent 'analysis' may undo the work of education and dissolve the associations it has set up. But, he argues, utilitarian morality is protected from this danger by being rooted in natural sentiment, in 'the social feelings of mankind', 'the desire to be in unity with our fellow-creatures'.

Throughout this chapter Mill reasonably insists that there is no *special* problem for utilitarian morality, as compared with any other system, in accounting for action in accordance with it.

His main contribution is his argument that there are internal as well as external sanctions for utilitarian morality. Action in accordance with the requirements of morality can be, in terms of a distinction he draws in the following chapter, a *part of* as well as a *means to* happiness. What begins as a more or less onerous means to some end that we desire may come to be desired for itself. Mill's illustration of this phenomenon is miserliness. A miser is one for whom money has ceased to be what it is for most men, an intrinsically uninteresting means to getting what they desire, and has become a thing desired for its own sake.

This is an unfortunate illustration since it is hard to conceive the miser's attitude to money as anything but a pathological aberration. The association of ideas often brings about the transference of an attitude, that is perfectly reasonable when adopted towards a certain thing, to something else associated with it in a striking way, which is not a reasonable object of the attitude in question. A person who has been very badly treated by a bearded man may come to fear and hate everyone who has a beard. But such associative transfers of emotion can be rational and life-enhancing, above all when they are connected with the discovery of new potentialities of satisfaction. An adolescent ploughs through D. H. Lawrence in pursuit of pornographic matter and comes to acquire a taste for writing that is more passionate, original and imaginative than the works of Ian Fleming. A man who settles down grimly to clearing a way from the front door of his house to the gate may come gradually to be entranced with horticulture. Liking what one gets can enlarge one's ability to get what one likes.

In fact it is unrealistic to suppose that the acquisition of a moral faculty, the development of conscientious feelings, is a kind of taste that is acquired by comparatively mature human beings. The foundations of the conscience, as Freud's theory of the super-ego contends, are laid very early in life. Approved conduct is chosen, against the pressure of instinctive impulses of selfishness and aggression, at an early stage of life as a means to the preservation of parental affection. The 'introjection' of parental commands that Freud speaks of is much the same thing as Mill's associative transfer of desire from end to means.

With maturity what Mill calls 'analysis' may tend to weaken the hold of this early conditioning. In effect, Mill's argument is that unreflective morality, authoritatively implanted in childhood, may be preserved in a new form when, with the achievement of reason, it is reconstructed on utilitarian foundations. The universal human need for a peaceable and co-operative society is better calculated to withstand the effects of rational criticism than the wishes of parents who no longer are so powerful and no longer seem so wise, or of a God whose existence may be doubtful.

(iv) THE PROOF OF THE PRINCIPLE OF UTILITY

Mill begins the handful of pages, as much discussed as any in moral philosophy, which he devotes to the proof of the principle of utility, by reiterating what he had said at the outset. 'Questions of ultimate ends are not amenable to direct proof,' but an 'equivalent to proof' is available. 'Considerations may be presented capable of determining the intellect either to give or to withhold its assent.'[44] Before we examine the considerations, supposedly equivalent to proof, that Mill presents there are two preliminary comments to be made.

The first is that Mill's thesis about the unprovable nature of ultimate ends is based on a very restricted conception of what could be admitted as a proof in this kind of case. 'Whatever can be proved to be good, must be so by being shown to be a means to something admitted to be good without proof.' If that is all that proof can be then it is a tautology that ultimate ends cannot be proved. That, whose goodness does not derive from the goodness of something else, cannot be shown to be good by deriving its goodness from that of something else.

To illustrate his point Mill says, 'the medical art is proved to be good by its conducing to health; but how is it possible to prove that health is good?'[45] One way in which the goodness of health could be proved is by showing that it is a necessary truth, arising from the fact that 'to be healthy' *means* 'to be in a good bodily condition'. First principles *can* be proved, by demonstration rather than by derivation from other truths of the same kind, provided that they are implicit definitions. The task of substantiating the underlying truths about meaning which render such first principles necessary is not likely to be simple. An appeal to intuition, or, less mysteriously, to the evident contradictoriness of the negation of the first principle in question, is almost bound to fail. If the necessity of the first principle had been obvious its truth would never have been put in question.

What has to be done is to develop the logical consequences of the assumption that the first principle under discussion is false until something whose contradictoriness is evident is reached. Alternatively, competing first principles have to be examined by applying them to circumstances in which acceptable consequences can be secured only if the original first principle is assumed. Mill is no doubt right in thinking that questions about ultimate ends are not amenable to *direct* proof. But that does not mean that they cannot be proved at all.

The second preliminary point is that the argument that Mill actually produces, with a view to 'determining the intellect either to give or to withhold its assent', is a proof, in a strict sense of the term, or, rather it is a deductive argument that would be a proof if its premises were true and the steps of reasoning it contains were valid. There is nothing at all roundabout or indirect about it, on the one hand, nor is it a matter of suggestion or persuasion, but has a strictly inferential form, on the other. Let us look at the argument itself.

Its first step is an affirmation of the principle of psychological hedonism: *pleasure, or happiness, is the only thing that men desire for its own sake*. The form in which this is put for the next stage of the argument is that each man (ultimately) desires nothing but his own pleasure. The second thesis may be called the principle of subjective ethical hedonism: *each man's pleasure is a good to him*. The connecting-link between this and the first principle is the claim that nothing can be desirable, or good, but what is actually desired. The final step in the argument is the derivation of the principle of objective ethical hedonism: *the general happiness is good for all*, which Mill sees as a direct consequence of the proposition that each man's happiness is a good, or the ultimate good, for him.

The third paragraph of Mill's fourth chapter suffices for the presentation of this argument. The remainder of the chapter is concerned to show that not only do men desire pleasure but that, in the end, they desire nothing else, that pleasure, or happiness, is the sole (ultimate) object of desire. His procedure here is to argue that all goods, or objects of desire, that appear to be distinct from pleasure or happiness are either means to it, and thus not ultimate objects of desire, or else are parts of happiness, in the sense discussed in the previous section. 'Whatever', he says, 'is desired otherwise than as a means to some end beyond itself, and ultimately to happiness, is desired as itself a part of happiness.'[46]

Mill's account of the status of his initial premise that pleasure alone is the ultimate object of desire is obscure. On the one hand he says that it is a fact of experience; on the other that 'desiring a thing and finding it pleasant . . . are phenomena entirely inseparable . . . two different modes of naming the same psychological fact'.[47] The first implies that it is a truth of empirical psychology, that could logically be false but in fact is not; the second that it is an analysis or conceptual truth, of the kind to which in his *System of Logic* he applied the phrase 'propositions merely verbal'. The same unresolved duality attaches to his concluding observation: 'to desire anything, except in proportion as the idea of it is pleasant, is a physical and metaphysical impossibility'.[48]

It will assist clarity at this point if two arguments that are commonly urged against Mill's first thesis are considered. Both rest on misunderstandings of his intent that are so unmitigatedly obvious that it is hard to credit the critics who exhibit them with both intellectual honesty and a minimum capacity for abstract reasoning. The first of them identifies pleasure with bodily pleasure, the lower quality of pleasure that Mill has laboured to distinguish from pleasure of a more elevated kind. On this interpretation Mill's thesis is a simple empirical falsehood. Bodily pleasure is, indeed, as nearly *universal* an object of desire as could be asked for. But it is quite obviously not the exclusive object of human desire. Men want power, status, achievement and a host of other things which have no essential bodily ingredient. This objection does not really deserve the name of criticism. It is a form of lazy abuse, no doubt expressive of thoughtless moral excitement, which merely discredits its proponents.

The second misunderstanding is rather more interesting. This maintains that it is not merely false that men desire only pleasure but that it is logically impossible that they should desire pleasure at all. What is desired is always some specific thing: a glass of wine, a good-looking woman, a peerage. The achievement of these objects is no doubt attended with pleasure, but it is the objects and not the pleasure that is desired. Why should it be supposed that the desire for some specific thing is not a desire for the pleasure that the thing can provide? After all what is desired is the thing in circumstances in which it will give pleasure. Suppose I have a desire for a glass of wine. More explicitly what I desire is to drink it. But that is not quite explicit enough. I shall not be satisfied if I am rendered unconscious and the wine is poured into my mouth and got down my throat while I am in that state.

It is true that all pleasure is pleasure from some fairly specific experience. There is no such thing as the enjoyment of pleasure by itself. A man who says 'Now I want some pleasure' but rejects every specific pleasant thing that is offered him – the coffee, the steak and kidney pudding, the swimming pool – not because he does not think that those particular things will please him, but because, he says, he wants pleasure in itself, uncontaminated by containment in any such concrete vehicle, is talking nonsense. Pleasure, one might say, is not a stuff but a relation. One can, of course, enjoy oneself and get pleasure without being able to say precisely what it is that is pleasing about one's situation. This will commonly happen when one is doing something so familiar as to seem intrinsically uninteresting, like combing one's hair or dressing, or something that is ordinarily taken to be more or less unpleasant, like washing up or shovelling manure. But even here one is not experiencing pleasure pure and simple, one is enjoying whatever the ordinarily uninteresting or disagreeable activity one is engaged upon is.

A man who seeks pleasure by itself and not the pleasure of something is like a business-man who seeks to reduce costs and yet who wants to do so without reducing the costs of any particular factor of production in his enterprise. But just as a business-man is efficient, in part, to the extent that he reduces costs, whatever they are the costs of, so an agent can desire pleasure, even if it is always the pleasure of some particular thing.

What perhaps lends some slight colour to this objection is Mill's tendency to say that men never desire anything but pleasure or that the ultimate object of desire is pleasure by itself. But these ways of speaking need not be taken in the absurd interpretation against which the objection is directed. If a specific pleasure-giving thing is logically implied by pleasure then to desire pleasure is necessarily also to desire some such thing. What Mill means by saying that nothing but pleasure is desired is that a thing cannot be desired unless it is conceived as pleasant. It is this that he holds to be a 'physical and metaphysical impossibility'.

Incidentally, at the point at which this phrase occurs, Mill identifies desiring a thing with the idea of it being pleasant. This is fairly clearly a slip. What a desire for something is, or at any rate necessarily implies, is the belief that the thing if obtained will be pleasing, is an idea of it, in other words, *as pleasant*. But that is very far from being the same thing as the thought or idea of the thing being itself pleasant. Whether or not the desire is itself pleasant will depend on the desirer's belief about the likelihood of its being satisfied. If his belief is that it is not in the least likely to be satisfied, then, the more pleasant he conceives the object of desire to be, the less pleasant, the more frustratedly painful, his desire for it will be.

This is a convenient point for a parenthetical comment on a related view which holds, not that the pursuit of pleasure is impossible, but that it is inevitably self-frustrating. Anyone, it has been said, who deliberately aims at pleasure is bound to be disappointed. Pleasure is, as a matter of psychological necessity, a by-product of the pursuit of other things for their own sakes. There is no doubt something to be said for this view, if pleasure is taken in its narrow, bodily sense. Intensely desired and intensely satisfying in the short run, bodily pleasures lack staying power. Few of those who can afford as much food and drink as they can physically contain accord them a very large place in their system of satisfactions. It is more common to make the pursuit of women a way of life but this would seem to owe its appeal to a great extent to its impurity from a bodily point of view. It is the pride of conquest, not sensuality, the power and the respect that he acquires, that keep Don Juan going. A harem would interest him no more than larders full of expensive food would gratify the person who likes to be seen at the best restaurants.

It is also true that many situations are pleasing only because they are spontaneous and unplanned. A car-trip designed like a major military operation may be oppressively dull. But there is no paradox in planning for unplanned pleasure. There are decisions, like where to stop for a picnic lunch, which can quite rationally be left to chance impulse. But, in general, it is rational to pursue pleasure and avoid its opposite deliberately. Provided that you can understand it, it is wiser to study the menu than to pick something at random.

There is a sense in which it is true that only pleasure is desired. To desire something is, in part, to conceive of it as something that will give pleasure. Expected pleasure is a logical shadow cast by desire. Or again, pleasure is the internal accusative of desire. It is important to see that the pleasure to which desire is logically or internally related is _expected_ pleasure. Desired objects often turn out not to be pleasant when achieved, or not to be as pleasant as was expected. In such cases it is rational to look for some feature of the circumstances which can explain the failure. If none can be found the failure should be noted, to modify the desire for that kind of thing in the future.

The initial premise of Mill's proof is, then, a tautology, in the only sense, at any rate, in which it is true. Furthermore, the sense of pleasure involved is the most inclusive and attenuated sense of the word that is possible. It seems unlikely, to say the least, that anything as controversial as the utilitarian principle could follow deductively from such a proposition together with a handful of other comparably uncontroversial assumptions.

But, in fact, the assumption which Mill invokes to arrive at the next stage of his proof is very far from uncontroversial. Universal execration has justly fallen on his view that only what is actually desired is desirable. Mill's critics uniformly and correctly observe that *desirable* means *ought to be desired* and not *can be desired*. It could further be objected that although the fact that something *is* desired is good, and, indeed, logically conclusive, evidence that it *can* be desired, the two are not, as Mill seems to suggest, one and the same (unless, which is perhaps the case, everything that it is possible to conceive as the object of a desire has been desired by somebody, somewhere).

What Mill attempts to do with this assumption is to establish a connection between desire and value. The excessively simple connection he asserts between them is that of identity. But the blatant unacceptability of his account of the connection does not mean that there is no logical relationship between them at all. It is a verbal truism that the desirable is of value; it is another that the desirable is that which ought to be desired. Could this last notion not be interpreted as *that which it would be rational to desire?* Now, considered in itself and without relation to other desires, the only feature of a desire which would expose it to criticism as regards its rationality is the necessarily implied belief that its object will, when achieved, yield satisfaction. One case, at any rate, in which a desire can be condemned as irrational is that in which the implied belief about the satisfyingness of its object is false. The obvious, paradigm instance of an irrational desire is one the achievement of whose object will prove displeasing to the agent. In the nature of the case this must be a fact he does not realise, for if he did the desire would disappear.

It might be objected that this conception of the rationality of a desire is merely prudential, that it identifies the desirable with that which a man ought, in prudence and for the sake of his own advantage, to desire. A partial reply to this objection is that in many cases it is to just this property of a situation that the word *desirable* is used to refer. When a house-agent describes a house as desirable or a doctor says that it is desirable for someone to winter in a warmer climate it is just this property that he has in mind. But it is a natural extension of the concept of the desirable to convert the prudential formula – that which would satisfy *anyone* – into the moral formula of utilitarianism – that which would satisfy *everyone*.

I have called this generalised or socialised concept of the desirable a 'natural extension' of the self-regarding or prudential concept. But a 'natural extension' is not an argument. A doubter might well regard it as a verbal confusion of a familiar kind about the two ordinary-language quantifiers 'anyone' and 'everyone'. Sometimes these terms can be substituted for each other without change of meaning, but sometimes they cannot. To borrow Quine's example: the affirmative sentences 'John can outrun anyone' and 'John can outrun everyone' mean the same; but their negations 'John cannot outrun anyone' and 'John cannot outrun everyone' very definitely do not.

It remains true, however, as C. I. Lewis has often insisted, that there is nothing peculiar or figurative about the use of such evaluative terms as 'ought' and 'good' in prudential discourse about the advantage of particular agents.[49] In discourse of this kind judgements of the desirability or value of things undoubtedly rest on their satisfyingness to those agents. Where the satisfaction involved is one which is universally felt the judgement can be expressed impersonally. To judge that such-and-such is a good car or headache-reliever is to assert that it would prove satisfying to anyone who wanted to own a car or relieve a headache. But sometimes the conditions of individual satisfaction differ as between one person and another: a woman who would make Smith very happy might do the opposite for

Jones and so would be a good wife for one but not for the other.

The prudential consideration of actions is concerned only with the satisfyingness or otherwise of those consequences to a particular agent. There are many actions all of whose significant consequences of this kind relate only to the particular agent. But equally there are many actions which contribute to or detract from the satisfaction of many people. It is these actions pre-eminently which are the field of application of moral judgement.

Now the conclusion that Mill reaches at the second stage of his proof of the principle of utility is that each man's happiness is a good to him. Although he bases it on the unacceptable assumption that what is good or desirable for a given person is simply what he desires, the conclusion can be given a more compelling basis. A man's prudential good is not what he does desire, I have argued, but what it would be rational for him to desire. In the first instance, this is what would in fact satisfy him, whether he realises it or not. Less restrictedly, it is what, through the totality of its consequences, yields the greatest satisfaction to the whole system of his likes and dislikes, his appetites and aversions. So, if the reasoning behind the second stage of Mill's argument is revised, it can be claimed on Mill's behalf that something amounting to a proof of a hedonistic principle of prudence is possible. The problem that remains is to justify the utilitarian account of the morally desirable as that which would yield satisfaction to *everyone*, corresponding to the account of the prudentially desirable as that which would yield satisfaction to anyone. It needs to be shown that this natural extension, as I have called it, of the concept of the desirable is a legitimate manœuvre and not the result of a failure to distinguish between the distributive and the collective ways of referring to people in general.

In the third and final stage of his proof Mill attempts to do this by arguing that since, as he claims to have shown, each man's happiness is a good to him, the general happiness is a good to all, to 'the aggregate of all persons', and thus is good in itself and without qualification. Here again a conclusion that is not in itself unreasonable is prejudiced by being derived in a hopelessly defective way. Mill, as is universally agreed, has committed a gross fallacy of composition. From *each man's X is Y to him* it simply does not follow that *every man's X is Y to everyone*. It certainly does not follow from the fact that each man's dreams are fascinating to him that everyone's dreams are fascinating to everyone. It would, perhaps, be possible, with a little strain, to take the word 'everyone' in the sentence 'everyone's dreams are fascinating to everyone' in a distributive sense, in which case it would be no more than an ungainly restatement of the premise. But that would not suffice for Mill's purpose. His final conclusion is that the *happiness of everyone, taken as a whole*, is a good to everyone. All that follows from the fact that each man finds his own dreams fascinating is that each man finds some part of the totality of men's dreams fascinating and that every part of that totality is fascinating to someone. Likewise the fact that each man's happiness is good to him implies only that each man finds some part of the general happiness good to him and that every part of the general happiness is good to someone. But what Mill wants to prove is that the general happiness, taken as a whole, is good to everyone.

One way in which moral philosophers have tried to do this is by giving a prudential answer to the question: why should I be moral? Men are social beings, both practically and emotionally. It is a practical or external condition of their well-being that they should be members of a happy community and, more particularly, a community that does not blame them for any of the unhappiness it suffers. It is also emotionally necessary to the happiness of most men, of all but the small minority of psychopaths who have failed to respond to moral education in childhood, that they should not know or think themselves to be responsible for the sufferings of others.

In other words, the general happiness is a good, a rational object of desire, to everyone, in view of the practical and emotional dependence of everyone on others. Now this familiar line of reasoning is rather generally thought to be insufficient. It seems to degrade morality by reducing it to mere policy, an insurance

67

against social disorder, revenge and guilt. To some extent this ignores the fact that the general happiness is an emotional as well as a practical condition of individual happiness or, in Mill's terms, that it is a part of individual happiness rather than a means to it, something internally as well as externally sanctioned. But even if this is borne in mind some further support seems necessary.

I think that there are three further considerations that can be adduced in support of the utilitarian principle that the general happiness, or something closely related to it, is the ultimate moral criterion. (1) The first of these arises from the problem of attempting to provide a criterion which will distinguish moral values and principles from values and principles of other kinds, such as prudential, technical, aesthetic or hygienic.[50] In recent times moral philosophers have followed Kant in offering formalistic solutions to this problem. The distinguishing feature of moral principles, it has been claimed, is that they are *universalisable*, in the sense that to apply them to anybody is implicitly to apply them to everybody, or *autonomous*, in that subscription to them must be freely chosen and not by submission to an external authority, or *overriding*, in that they are supreme in any case where they come into conflict with principles of other kinds.

I believe that all of these three formal criteria of morality are inadequate. Certainly all moral principles are universalisable, but then so are all other rational prescriptions for or recommendations of conduct. If I ought prudentially to save some of my income then so ought everyone else placed as I am. Universalisability is a necessary, but not a sufficient, condition of the moral status of a principle. Autonomy is an obscure requirement. If it means that a principle is not moral unless it is a creative innovation on the part of its exponent then it is not peculiar to morality, for there are technical innovations, nor is it a necessary condition of the morality of a principle of conduct, unless no docile conformist could be a moral agent. If it means the sincere endorsement of professed principles then it is just as applicable in the other, non-moral fields of conduct. There is also obscurity about the interpretation of overridingness. Does it mean that a principle is moral if and only if it *does in fact* prevail over principles with conflicting implications for conduct or if and only if it *should* do so. The first view leads to wildly counter-intuitive results, for example, that a man who prudently restrains his charitable impulses does not accept charity as a moral obligation. The second view involves a vicious circularity.[51]

In the face of these difficulties a material criterion of morality, in terms of its subject-matter, is plainly indicated. What material aspect of actions makes them liable to moral consideration? Generally, it would seem their bearing, favourable or unfavourable, on the interests, happiness or welfare of the people affected by the actions in question.

(2) This conclusion is supported by some rather obvious, if diffuse, empirical facts about what is ordinarily regarded as morality. Most codes of conduct that are unreflectively recognised as moral prohibit, with occasional exceptions, killing, injuring or inflicting physical pain on other people, taking their property, telling them lies, breaking promises made to them. Now all of these are actions which are calculated, if not by logic then by the most obvious and irresistible causality, to cause suffering. Most such codes also call for active benevolence, at least to the extent of alleviating suffering, if not of positively augmenting existing happiness.

Not only does a negatively utilitarian conception of the ultimate moral end, as the prevention of suffering, cover most of the broad principles which would commonsensically be held to be the foundation of a moral code. It also explains the exceptions that are customarily admitted to these broad principles. Killing is permitted for self-defence, in war or as legal execution. The property of others can be appropriated in an emergency. The duties of truth-telling and promise-keeping can be overridden if it is plain that much more suffering will ensue if they are kept than if they are broken.

(3) Essentially the same point is made by an inference it is natural to draw from the fact of the temporal and spatial variety of moral convictions. It is notorious that conflicting moral ideas

prevail in communities that are historically or geographically distinct from each other. Once madmen were beaten. The purpose was the utilitarian one of rendering them sane again. The means adopted were appropriate to the false belief that madmen were possessed by demons, who were expected to vacate a physical container that was being beaten. Those who come to think of this theory of demonic possession as false replace the flail as therapeutic instrument by the analyst's couch. In either case the underlying reasoning is utilitarian.

Eskimoes, we are told, endorse euthanasia of the unproductively aged. In a society living at the very margin of subsistence the survival of all has to be bought at the cost of the lives of some. Those who cannot now or in the future make any contribution to what is necessary for the society's survival are the natural candidates for sacrifice. Utility selects them as those whose going will bring about the smallest overall loss of welfare.

The hard core of morality, then, as it is ordinarily conceived, is utilitarian in character, at least negatively. Furthermore, the theory that the principle of utility is fundamental to morals affords, in conjunction with the manifest differences of belief that there are about the causes of happiness and suffering and of circumstances in which actions and their hedonic consequences are differently related, a coherent explanation of many of the differences of moral opinion as between differently informed or circumstanced societies. It is also a considerably more plausible reaction to the fact of large-scale moral disagreement than the subjectivist conclusion that ultimate moral convictions are simply a matter of brute, unarguable preference.

Mill's 'proof' of the principle of utility is by no means the tissue of errors most of its critics have supposed. Much of it is defensible as it stands: that the object of desire, and thus of action, is expected pleasure and that there is an intimate connection between value and desire, in that what is good for a person is what he would desire if he were rational, namely that which being really pleasant, would fulfil the expectations of pleasure which, in desiring it, he ascribes to it. The weakest point is the transition from this latter conclusion to the utilitarian principle itself, that the good of all is really identical with the good of each. The argument from the external sanctions of morality shows that the good of all is a *causal condition* of the good of each. It is hard to be happy in a generally miserable society and individual happiness in such circumstances is likely to be very insecure, especially if the individual in question comes to be seen by his fellows as responsible for some of their misery. The argument from internal sanctions shows that the good of all is *part* of the good of each. We have an intense interest in the welfare of some other people and some direct interest in the welfare of nearly everyone. What has not been shown is that the good of all is the total, ultimate and overriding good of each. But this, for all the lip-service that is paid to it, is a very extreme and millennial belief. Its truth is not necessary to substantiate the hard, common-sensical core of morality, for this does not require that we should devote ourselves in a totally disinterested way to the general welfare but, more modestly, that we should abstain from positive injury to others and, perhaps, alleviate their sufferings where it is not too prejudicial to our own welfare to do so. For this more restricted policy each of us has good and sufficient reasons of interest, externally sanctioned. The morally heroic or supererogatory conduct of the saint is rational only for those whose direct concern for the welfare of others is of a scope and intensity which are not to be found in the structure of interests derived from the innate constitution and moral education of most of us.

(v) JUSTICE AND UTILITY

The most persistent objection to the claim of utilitarianism to impart rationality and coherence to ordinary moral beliefs is that it fails to substantiate our unreflective convictions about justice. The point can be made more forcefully. There are principles of justice, it may be held, which are at once more certain or self-evident than the principle of utility and yet which are not compatible with it. Mill addresses himself to this problem in the fifth and concluding chapter of *Utilitarianism*. His discussion has many merits. It covers a great deal of ground, especially in elaborating the various more or less distinct ideas which the word 'justice' has been used to convey. But he does not really engage himself fully and satisfactorily with the main difficulties that common convictions about justice put in the way of the position he is defending.

These difficulties are two in number. The first concerns distribution. The principle of utility, it is objected, evaluates actions only by reference to the total amount of good or evil, pleasure or pain, that they produce. But, the objection continues, it is intuitively obvious that two actions which bring about resulting situations that are identical in the overall balance of good and evil they contain will differ very markedly in value if, for example, the good and evil involved are equally distributed in one case but very unequally distributed in the other.

The second difficulty concerns rules. It is objected that two actions that produce identical overall amounts of good and evil will differ in value if one involves the breach of a rule, such as that of promise-keeping or truth-telling, but the other does not.

In his discussion of justice Mill does have a little to say about the problem of distribution, making the rather perfunctory claim that it is catered for by Bentham's formulation of the greatest happiness principle. The reference to the happiness of the greatest number in that formulation, Mill contends, secures the equality of treatment on which the exponents of justice insist. But he does not have anything to say here about the problem of rules and it may be reasonably complained that, for all its merits, his chapter on the subject never really takes the measure of the difficulties which the notion of justice presents to the utilitarian.

The issues Mill does concern himself with are somewhat tangential to the more serious difficulties. First, he considers the objection that there is a direct conflict between justice and the utilitarians' *summum bonum*: expediency. At this level of generality it is easy enough for him to dismiss the conflict as merely verbal.

He can freely admit that there are frequent divergences between the claims of justice and personal or individual expediency, which is what we usually have in mind when we use the word. But the expediency which the utilitarian regards as the ultimate moral criterion is not personal but public; it is the general happiness and not individual advantage. This fails to meet the point that there are apparent conflicts between justice and what is *socially* expedient, to take a familiar example, the exemplary punishment of an innocent man.

His second, and principal, concern is the claim that there is a natural or instinctive sense of justice which yields injunctions incompatible with those implied by the principle of utility. Since he admits that even if it were natural and instinctive that would not imply the validity of its pronouncements, his attempt to show that it is nevertheless explainable in terms of self-preservative and sympathetic impulses, which are acknowledged by the utilitarian theory of human nature and which constitute the psychological foundation of the principle of utility itself, is lacking in theoretical interest.

Mill discerns five different notions of justice: (1) respect for legal rights, (2) respect for moral rights, the rights accorded by an ideal system of law, (3) distribution in accordance with desert, (4) keeping faith or fulfilling reasonable and justified expectations and (5) impartiality. He sees that the idea of equality is intimately associated with that of justice and suggests, on etymological grounds, that the basic notion of justice, underlying its varied specific senses, is that of conformity to law, actual or ideal.

He then goes on to argue that the distinction between the obligations of justice and the other obligations of morality more or less coincides with that traditionally drawn by moralists between perfect duties, which are correlative to a right possessed by a particular individual, and imperfect duties, such as that of charity, which are not. The perfect obligations of justice, he goes on, are the most important part of justice. What they are chiefly concerned with is abstention from doing harm to others, either by aggression against the persons or property of other people or by failure to comply with their justified expectations about one's conduct in relation to them, as in breaking promises and telling lies. What makes these obligations the most important that there are is that the ordinary person's power to affect the welfare of his own fellow-men is largely confined to the field that they cover.

Although there is much to be said for Mill's view that abstention from acts that would harm others is the most important part of morality, the point has nothing very much to do with justice. Murder, assault, theft, lying and promise-breaking are ordinarily (or, in the case of murder and theft, necessarily) wrong. They are, indeed, invasions or floutings of the rights of their victims, but they are not exactly unjust, at any rate in the current sense of that word, any more than incest, the favourite example of an act, which though morally wrong, is not unjust. What is primarily wrong with murder is that a man is *killed*, not that *he*, rather than somebody else, is.

Justice, as we understand it and in the sense in which it is commonly alleged to be unprovided for by utilitarianism, is first and foremost a distributive notion. It applies primarily to the comparative allocation of benefits and burdens as between different people. The simplest criterion of justice is equality. But its simplicity is somewhat spurious: different concrete modes of treating people can each make a claim to being truly equal treatment. As Mill himself observes, communists, who agree that there ought to be equality of incomes, disagree as to what precisely this equality consists in. Is it a matter of strictly identical income for each person or of proportioning income to needs or of proportioning income to the individual's productive contribution to the pool from which income is distributed? More generally, Mill makes the point that the requirements of justice are no less controversial than those of utility. He cites income-distribution, taxation and punishment as practices or institutions whose just administration is a matter of persistent dispute. Should taxation, for example, be a fixed proportion of income or should it be graduated so that the rich pay a higher rate of tax or should it be the same for all, the services of government being conceived like any other marketable good?[52]

Mill's claim that the intuitive demand for equality of treatment is sufficiently catered for by Bentham's reference to 'the greatest number' in his formulation of the principle of utility is unconvincing. If anything it draws attention to a defect in that formulation. Suppose that one of two alternative actions causes a large amount of happiness to a small number of people while the other produces a smaller aggregate of happiness but distributes it more widely. Bentham's formula suggests at least that the aggregate happiness involved in the two outcomes is not decisive, that it has to be balanced against width of distribution for a final evaluation. In fact what Bentham seems to have intended is that the criterion of value is the happiness of everyone affected. This does provide a minimal equality of treatment: an adequate evaluation of an action must take into account the happiness or suffering of all who are affected by it. Does the utilitarian principle, thus interpreted, have any further implications about the proper distribution of good and evil?

I believe it has. This can best be shown by considering the most naïve way in which the supposed indifference of utilitarianism to the distribution of good and evil is argued for. Suppose, the objection runs, that there are a hundred people and a hundred units of utility or value to distribute. The principle of utility supplies no ground for preferring an allocation of one unit to each person over an allocation of the hundred units to one lucky man and of nothing at all to the other ninety-nine. The mistake in this argument is its assumption that the utility accruing from the distribution of some good is independent of the manner of its distribution. But this is obviously false. We do not distribute utilities of fixed value, in fact, but concrete things such as oranges, medals and so forth which will have different utilities depending on the way in which they are distributed.

In most imaginable circumstances the distribution of a hundred oranges among a hundred people that will bring about the largest total utility is that in which each person gets only one. Like most objects of desire oranges are subject to the law of diminishing marginal utility. The second orange that a man eats at a particular time is ordinarily going to satisfy him less than the first did. This is, broadly speaking, a consequence of the finite satisfiability of desire. If the desire for a given kind of thing within a given period is finitely satisfiable there must be a finite amount of that thing which will wholly extinguish the desire for it and whose final or marginal portion will yield no satisfaction at all. Provided that the curve which describes the satisfactions yielded by successive increments of the good in question, from the first, and positively satisfying, one to the last and neutral one is regular and without major changes of direction there will be a continuous decrease of satisfaction accruing from one point on the curve to the next.

It follows that if two men get much the same satisfaction from the first orange they are given and that for both the marginal utility of oranges steadily diminishes at much the same rate the greatest total utility will be achieved by giving them one orange each rather than by giving two oranges to either of them. Only if giving a second orange to either yields more satisfaction than giving a first orange to the other will equal distribution produce less overall satisfaction than one of the other, partial, possibilities. That would be the case only if there was a very considerable difference between the utilities of a first orange to the two men or if there was some difference of this kind and also a much smaller diminution of utility in the case of the man whose first orange had the higher utility.

Under this abstract, but not unnatural, assumption, then, the principle of utility strictly implies arithmetical or external equality of distribution as the necessary means for the maximisation of overall satisfaction. If that sort of equality is what is required by men's intuitions about justice then utilitarianism, within the limits set by the assumption about the conditions of satisfaction, endorses it. But although arithmetical equality of distribution is the criterion of justice that recommends itself to the first unreflective glance of moral intuition, qualifications suggest themselves on second thoughts. The first of these is the principle that men's differing *needs* must be taken into account if just distribution is to be assured. There is, it could be argued, no injustice in giving both of two oranges to a man who is starving, even when there is another man about who is mildly interested in having an orange although he has just had a substantial meal. A second widely supported departure from raw equality takes account of men's differing *deserts*. If a man has laboriously tended a small orange tree on which two oranges have finally come to fruition it would be no injustice if he were to eat both of them and not give half his crop to another man who happens to be passing by at the time when it becomes ripe.

Now both of these departures from bare, external equality are implied by the principle of utility since in each case the assumptions about the satisfaction-patterns or utility-schedules of the men involved, which must be correct if the principle is to entail external equality of distribution, are not correct. In the case of differing needs the utility to the starving man of a second orange will be much greater than that of a first orange to the man who has just eaten. In the case of differing deserts a larger set of utilities is relevant. The laborious cultivator has incurred a good deal of disutility through his labour which the passer-by has not had to undergo. To bring him up to the normal level of satisfaction, which the passer-by may be presumed to enjoy, he needs both oranges. Or, less figuratively, the generally lower level of satisfaction of the orange-tender implies that a second orange will provide him with more utility than a first orange would provide for the passer-by.

In these two cases, then, there are differences between the satisfaction-patterns of the individuals involved which, if the principle of utility is accepted, imply precisely the departures from strict, external equality that reflective moral intuition requires if just distribution is to be assured. Utilitarianism provides here a connected and systematic derivation of widely-recognised principles of justice that the intuitionist must, it seems, lay down

77

as an unrelated set of axioms, or dogmas, of just distribution. The situation looks much like that which prevails with regard to right action in general. Utilitarianism presents generally acknowledged principles of right action in a systematic way, although it deprives them of their supposedly absolute and exceptionless character; intuitionism can only assert the principles singly and without connection to each other, a fact which gives rise to the problem of the conflict of duties.

However, in the case of justice, the intuitionist can argue that the three principles of external equality, needs and deserts are not as disconnected as they may seem. For the two departures from *external* equality, that is equality in respect of the objective, physical amount of the good distributed, are both justifiable on egalitarian grounds. Each of them is invoked in circumstances where some peculiarity in the satisfaction-patterns of the beneficiaries (or, of course, burden-bearers, where something of negative utility is being distributed) causes there to be an incongruity between the objective amount distributed and the satisfaction experienced as a result of the distribution. Where men's satisfaction-patterns are much the same, in both level and shape, so to speak, external equality will produce equal satisfaction. Where they are not, equality of satisfaction can be secured only if there is some inequality of external distribution. So the intuitive egalitarian can claim that his fundamental criterion of justice, now restated as that of equality of experienced satisfaction, connects and systematises the three specific principles of justice as well as utilitarianism does, even if it takes equality to be axiomatically just and does not derive it from a further principle. Such an egalitarianism of satisfaction is, indeed, hedonistic in what it regards as the value to be equally distributed. But by detaching equality from maximisation it is not utilitarian.

The egalitarian can argue further that utilitarianism has additional implications about right distribution which are directly incompatible with intuitive notions of justice. In a perfectly competitive economic system people are rewarded in accordance with their achievements; the more they contribute to the total output of utility the larger their income. Such a system is rational from a utility-maximising point of view because it provides inducements to ensure that those with special productive capacities go into the type of employment in which their largest possible contribution to the total stock of utility is realised. This method of income-distribution must be the best one to the strict utilitarian: any departure from it will reduce the total amount of utility made available by the system.

The practice of rewarding people in proportion to the services they actually render in augmenting utility is often described as one of treating them in accordance with their deserts. But what people deserve in the light of the results they achieve is not generally the same as what they deserve in the light of their efforts. A popular singer may intensely gratify a vast number of people at the cost of no disutility to himself at all, if, as may well be the case, he would prefer to be singing to a crowd of enraptured devotees than to be doing anything else. An unpopular epic poet, on the other hand, may toil in the most painful and arduous fashion to produce a huge, unreadable work which pleases neither him nor anyone else.

A system of rewarding people in accordance with their differing natural endowments in the way of utility-producing capacity seems unjust since it simply reflects the 'natural injustice' with which the innate power to be socially useful is distributed. It may often be true that under such a system even the worst off will be absolutely better off than they would be under a system in which everyone was allotted an equal share of the total stock of utility produced, but in which, because of the 'irrational' allocation of people to particular jobs, the total stock in question would be a small one. But the latter is a very extreme alternative to a perfectly competitive system. There are many intermediate possibilities in which an incomplete approach to equality of income could be achieved without much diminution of the total output of utility. It is these intermediate possibilities that the technique of redistributive taxation seeks to exploit.

It should be stressed that although utilitarianism endorses maximisation it is maximisation of utility that it is concerned with and not maximisation of output of typically utility-bearing things. It does not, therefore, endorse unqualified enlargement of the Gross National Product, although the G.N.P. is, no doubt, the most accessible measure of the total stock of utility produced by a social-economic system. Nevertheless it does seem to imply that unequal natural gifts should be unequally rewarded for the sake of maximisation and thus that the best method of distribution is not necessarily that which is intuitively the justest.

There is a possible defence to which the utilitarian could appeal at this point which develops the analogy that has already been mentioned, and shown to be imperfect, between the principles of justice and the principles of right conduct generally. On the whole utilitarianism is in favour of honesty. By and large the fact that an action is honest is a sufficient reason for thinking that it is right. But, for the utilitarian, the rightness of honesty is not absolute and unconditional. He recognises that there are circumstances in which the honest thing to do is not the right thing to do, because, for example, it would cause pain or endanger the state. Similarly, he could argue, the fact that an action or practice is just, in the intuitive sense that has been examined, is generally a sufficient reason for taking it to be right. But its rightness may be no more absolute and unconditional than that of honesty. Let justice be done, he says, as long as it does not make the heavens fall.

There are good utilitarian grounds for thinking that a method of distribution which aims to bring about equality of satisfaction will generally secure the maximisation of utility, the grounds provided by the utilitarian defence of the principles of external equality, needs and deserts, in the sense of compensation for disutility incurred. But it also allows that there can be good reason for departures from just distribution so defined. The recognition of desert in the sense of reward for services actually rendered may be required for the overall maximisation of utility, even if the worst-off are not absolutely better-off in the service-rewarding system.

In fact, of course, nearly everywhere men live under systems in which income and property are very unequally distributed and also, presumably, satisfaction, though, to a lesser extent, no doubt. In assessing the effects of any move towards equality in such a system we need to consider not merely the pattern of satisfactions that would prevail once the new system was established but also the effects of the transition itself. To this Hume's point about fixed expectations is relevant: 'It would be greater cruelty to dispossess a man of any thing, than not to give it to him'.[53] This does not mean that utilitarianism excludes social-economic reforms of an equalising tendency but it does imply that they should be gradual and achieved by redistributive taxation rather than outright expropriation.

At the present time the alleged inadequacies of the utilitarian theory of justice is the main theme of the destructive criticism that is brought to bear on the doctrine. It replaces in this role the objection that utilitarianism commits the 'naturalistic fallacy' which was itself the successor to the criticism that its hedonist criterion of value was immorally degraded. This discussion has done no more than outline some of the main points at issue in the controversy and certainly does not pretend to have resolved it. What does seem clear is that justice is less easily accounted for by utilitarianism than Mill supposed.

IV. FOUR CRITICS

Mill's *Utilitarianism* first appeared as a series of articles in *Fraser's Magazine* in the latter part of 1861. Two years later these were republished as a book. For the next forty years, until the publication in 1903 of G. E. Moore's *Principia Ethica*, they remained the authoritative exposition of a major option in ethical theory and attracted serious criticism as such. Moore's examination of Mill's doctrine had the effect, for reasons it is now not easy to discern, of converting utilitarianism, in the view of prevailing philosophical opinion, into an exemplary tissue of error. It was not until the widespread rejection of Moore's antinaturalism in the last couple of decades that Mill's doctrine recovered its status as a genuine theoretical possibility and, with this, came to receive once again the kind of criticism that does not presuppose, from the outset, that it is fundamentally misguided.

Four critics stand out in the period 1863 to 1903 by reason of the intrinsic interest or actual influence of their objections to utilitarianism. The first of these is John Grote, Whewell's successor in the Knightbridge chair at Cambridge and younger brother of the historian of Greece. His *Examination of the Utilitarian Philosophy* was written as Mill's articles first appeared and was published in 1870, four years after its author's death. Grote's pupil, Henry Sidgwick, was much more sympathetic to Mill. His massively thorough and scrupulous *Methods of Ethics* was first published in 1874. Although more utilitarian than anything else, the book is wholly explicit about its departures from Benthamite orthodoxy in contrast to the defensive and unacknowledged character of Mill's own revisions to his ethical inheritance. Two years later in 1876 F. H. Bradley published his *Ethical Studies,* the long third chapter of which, 'Pleasure for Pleasure's Sake', is a violently polemical assault on Mill's position.

Finally, and most lethally for utilitarianism, Moore's *Principia Ethica* in 1903, despite its heavy dependence on Sidgwick and its unreflective confidence that the rightness of actions is self-evidently determined by the goodness of their consequences, provided, in its critique of naturalism and in its detailed objections to Mill's views in its third chapter, the means with which utilitarianism was largely deprived of serious discussion, let alone positive development, for half a century.

(i) JOHN GROTE

Grote's *Examination of the Utilitarian Philosophy* was not, according to his editor, originally intended for publication but rather for the purpose of clarifying his ideas on the subject for himself. The fact may explain the somewhat desultory and repetitive nature of the book. It also renders all the more creditable its consistently gracious tone which is in the greatest possible contrast to the abusiveness of most of Mill's critics, a feature which attains its most extreme development in Bradley.

A persistent theme in Grote's criticism of Mill is his dissatisfaction with the claim of utilitarianism to be a pre-eminently *scientific* ethical theory. An adequate moral philosophy must, as he puts it, be idealist and not positivist. There is an essential imperativeness about virtue. There would seem to be a number of distinct points in a state of unresolved confusion here. In the first place he seems to be saying that conclusions about what is morally imperative cannot be validly derived from empirical facts about human nature and conduct, that there is no logical connection between what ought to be and what is. To the extent that utilitarians try to deduce the greatest happiness principle, as Mill does in his 'proof', from psychological hedonism they are exposed to this criticism, at least in so far as their psychological premise is, or is taken by them to be, an empirical generalisation. But, secondly, Grote denies that there can be a science of the kind of free action that must occur if morality is to have any application. A third point is that Grote is dissatisfied with the kind of ideal that utilitarianism, for all its empirical pretensions, has to assume. Happiness is too passive an end. The positive improvement of human character, through, for example, self-control, is an essential ingredient in an adequate morality. The facts, then, to which utilitarianism appeals in support of the greatest happiness principle do not have the logical capacity to establish it. That principle, as Grote puts it, is not empirical and inductive; it is *a priori*. What is more, the facts in question are not available; there are no laws of free action. Finally, the ideal that utilitarianism inevitably does adopt fails to recognise the true nature of virtue by defining it in terms of happiness.

Grote's well-taken point that the utilitarian principle is *a priori* does not undermine the claim of utilitarianism to be empirical and inductive as radically as he supposes. Where the intuitionist has to invoke a multitude of non-empirical intuitions of rightness, the utilitarian derives all his specific, detailed moral principles, with the aid of the greatest happiness principle, from empirical generalisations about the consequences of action. There is a parallel with natural science here. Science is not rendered un-empirical by the conception that singular observations yield theories only with the aid of a non-empirical inductive principle, neither need morality be if it is taken to involve an analogous dependence on the non-empirical principle that right actions augment the general happiness. If Mill wrongly supposed that the utilitarian principle is an empirical generalisation, he was equally wrong about the law of universal causation, which he took to be the indispensable foundation of scientific, eliminative induction.

Moving on from this more or less methodological issue, Grote says that there are two main deficiencies in utilitarianism. The first is its account of the right distribution of happiness, of who it is that actions, if they are to be right, are to be useful to. The second is its account of happiness itself. On the matter of distribution Grote's position is the conservative opposite of the type of egalitarian criticism of the utilitarian theory of justice considered in the last section of the chapter on Mill. Grote takes utilitarianism to entail the strictly equal distribution of happiness, a very questionable assumption, as I have shown, and objects that this is altogether too abstract, mechanical and unfeeling. It ignores, in his view, the special moral claims of those to whom the moral agent is specially related, a point of view dramatically represented in Godwin's hypothetical decision, on grounds of public utility, to rescue Archbishop Fenelon rather than his grandmother from a burning building. Duty, Grote maintains, is particular before it is general. He dismisses Mill's utilitarian justification of the priority of the moral claims of those to whom agents are specially related, in terms of the painful disappointment of expectations the neglect of those claims would involve, as being 'not really utilitarian'. As it stands this a very weak objection. In such cases the expectations really exist and must be taken into account in the evaluation of consequences. If Grote had argued that, in a world of utilitarians, such expectations ought not to exist, he could have gone on to argue that, with the dissemination of utilitarianism, special, relative duties might evaporate. But, first, that is not the situation that we are actually in, as far as actual expectations are concerned, and, secondly, even in a world of utilitarians there would be good arguments of effectiveness for the position that charity begins at home.

On the question of the kind of happiness which utilitarianism takes as its ideal Grote is too honourable a controversialist to indulge in comminations of animal sensuality. He objects that Mill hovers between idealist and positivist conceptions of happiness, between defining it as what men should desire and as what men do desire. In fact, I think it is fairly clear that Mill takes happiness to be the former: *actual* or realised happiness, in other words, as against (perhaps mistakenly) *expected* happiness. In this connection, discussing Mill's unfortunate distinction between different qualities of pleasure, Grote neatly argues that Mill's criterion in terms of the preference of qualified judges is in fact quantitative, since in simply preferring 'higher' to 'lower' pleasures the judges are simply asserting the former to be *more* pleasurable.

Discussing Mill's proof Grote sees that, in Mill's interpretation of the words involved, the proposition that men desire only pleasure is trivially true. He thus rightly concentrates his criticism on Mill's naïvely invalid deduction from this truth of the conclusion that pleasure is ideally desirable, and on the fallacious generalisation by which he moves from the premise that each man desires his own happiness to the conclusion that everyone desires the happiness of all.

His fundamental difference with Mill here concerns the utilitarian subordination of virtue to happiness. On the one hand he has an unarguable primary conviction that virtue has an intrinsic value of its own and not merely as a human disposition contributory to the general happiness. On the other he is dissatisfied with Mill's theory of moral motivation, of his account of how the general happiness can become an operative end for the individual.

On the first point Grote himself denies the value of asceticism or self-sacrifice for its own sake, that is to say, of pointless asceticism, which makes no contribution to happiness. It is thus a little hard to see what, apart from a certain instinctive moral decorum, prevents him from agreeing that virtue derives its value from the contribution to happiness which it is, of all things, the most calculated to make. In this connection it is worth noticing a distinction he draws between duty, which he sees as, so to speak, negatively prompted by conscience, by fear of guilt, and virtue, which he regards as altogether more spontaneous, a finite analogue of the overflowing of divine grace, expressive of a constitutional benevolence, the genial, rather than the stern, daughter of the voice of God. His difference from Mill here is very elusive, almost a matter of tone.

As for Mill's account of the motives of morality, of how it is that men come to find pleasure in the pursuit of the general happiness and make it a direct end of conduct, Grote holds that this is one of the two respects, along with his misguided distinction between different qualities of pleasure, in which Mill represents a radical departure from orthodox utilitarianism as no more than the removal of a prevalent misunderstanding of it. Certainly Mill does emphasise the internal sanction of morality, founded on sympathy and 'social feeling', as well as the external sanctions enumerated by Bentham: physical, political, 'moral or popular' and religious. But what Mill identifies as an internal sanction Bentham acknowledges in a different way, as one of the simple pleasures (number eight in fact), the pleasure of benevolence and good-will. Grote agrees with what is implicit in Bentham's practice here, the view that sanctions must be external to the agent, and then, insisting that morality is an internal phenomenon, concludes that Mill should not have treated sympathy as a sanction and that sanctions cannot account for morally right conduct. This is at best a verbal point. Bentham and Mill both recognise sympathy or natural benevolence as an explanation of right conduct. Mill, perhaps figuratively, calls it a sanction and Bentham does not. Grote prefers Bentham's terminology but fails to see that Bentham, as much as Mill, if with less ceremony, provides an internal determinant of moral action.

(ii) HENRY SIDGWICK

It may seem odd to treat Sidgwick as a critic of utilitarianism, rather than as a continuator of it. As was said earlier, his *Methods of Ethics* is more utilitarian than anything else, for all its large admixture of intuitionism, and, if he has to be categorised definitely under one head, it must be as a utilitarian. For all his qualifications he does remain an unwavering ethical hedonist. The ultimate good is, in his view, 'desirable consciousness' and this, he argues, cannot be anything but happiness, conceived in the traditional utilitarian way, as a sum of pleasures. The repugnance this conclusion tends to excite at a first glance he explains away as the result of a set of mutually reinforcing misunderstandings. Pleasure gets confused with animal pleasure; much pleasure occurs only because it has not been consciously sought; the pleasure in question is thought to be that of the agent and not that of all.

But Sidgwick differs from the classical utilitarianism on four major points. In the first place, he is not a psychological hedonist. Pleasure, conceived as 'agreeable feeling', is not, experience shows, the sole object of desire. He lays stress here on the point just mentioned, that much pleasure can be attained only if it is not consciously pursued. Even if psychological hedonism were true it would not imply the greatest happiness principle. Sidgwick firmly rejects Mill's proof.

Secondly, benevolence, the pursuit of happiness in general, is not enough. To start with, the happiness that is relevant to morality is not just that of human beings, but that of the whole sentient creation, of every being that is capable of happiness or its opposite. Sidgwick raises the question, which has become much more pressing with the advances in reproductive technology since his time, of whether we should aim at the greatest *total* happiness or the greatest *average* happiness, given that the actual number of sentient beings is something that is to some extent dependent on our voluntary decisions. Should one have four children who attain six units of happiness each or five children who attain five? But his main point here is that not only must we increase the happiness of others, we must ensure that happiness is rightly distributed. He concludes that equal distribution is the principle of just distribution that recommends itself to reason but that it is not a consequence of the, equally rational, principle of benevolence itself.

Sidgwick's third main departure from standard utilitarianism arises from his belief that prudence, the maximisation by the individual agent of his own happiness in the long run, is as intuitively evident as benevolence, but that there is no guarantee that the dictates of these two principles will coincide. Benevolence calls for acts of self-sacrifice for which there is no earthly recompense in prudential terms. The only way in which duty and interest can be reconciled is by the activities of a divine governor of the universe, distributing rewards and punishments, an echo of one of Kant's postulates of practical reason. Sidgwick's religious doubts led him to resign his Cambridge fellowship early in his career. Even if they concerned the Thirty-nine Articles, rather than the existence of God, and although he thought belief in God natural to men, he did not think that belief provable. This disquiet about the availability of that without which the equally imperative claims of prudence and rational benevolence could not be harmonised may be thought to underlie his long and intense interest in psychical research.

Finally, Sidgwick departs most radically from standard utilitarianism in his theory of moral knowledge. On the one hand, for reasons that were later to be less cogently but more influentially stated by Moore, he was convinced that the first principle or principles of morality could not be true by definition or analytic.[54] On the other hand they seemed to possess a degree of certitude which they could not have if merely empirical, since, as highly general, they would then have to be inductions. They are, then, substantive or synthetic, but at the same time *a priori*. The only way in which they could be known is by intuition, which, in view of the generality of its deliverances, is better described as reason than as sense.

Sidgwick lays down four criteria for the validity of moral, or other, intuition.[55] It must be expressed in clear and precise terms; it must be self-evident to reflective attention; it must be consistent with other deliverances of intuition; it must be endorsed by the general agreement of experts about it. By these criteria, Sidgwick argues, the moral first principles of commonsense intuitionism are a failure. Exceptions can always be found to absolute specific principles of duty such as those that enjoin truth-telling and promise-keeping. Such principles typically can conflict. If amended and qualified to cover such exceptions and conflicts they become too complex to be intuited and the work of amendment is not completable anyway.

There are principles, however, which, according to Sidgwick, do pass his four tests.[56] The most important of these are, first, two somewhat tautologous-looking formal principles: that what is right for one person is also right for others similarly circumstanced and that general rules should be applied impartially.

Rather more substantial is the principle, integral to prudence, that there should be an equal concern for all the temporal parts of conscious life, in other words that future goods should be treated as on a level with present good, with due allowance for the lesser certainty of the former. Then there is the principle that the good of one individual is 'no better from the point of view of the Universe', and, therefore, to the eye of reason, than that of any other. Finally, there is the principle that makes goodness effective for conduct, that a rational being ought to aim at realising good. The last two put together amount to what Sidgwick calls the principle of rational benevolence and, if good is interpreted in his way as happiness, an improved, rationalised, version of the fundamental principle of utilitarianism is achieved. Sidgwick adds in confirmation of the intuitive and self-evident status of this principle that it is, empirically, the touchstone by reference to which conflicts between the more specific principles of common-sense morality are adjudicated. Furthermore, to the extent to which they are deserving of acceptance, these common-sense principles are themselves implications, in the light of empirical knowledge about the consequences of action, of the principle of rational benevolence. It follows that an amended utilitarianism coincides with the findings of intuitionism, at least to the extent that it is rationally to be expected that it should.

Two specific points remain to be mentioned. Sidgwick is much more of a moral conservative than Bentham or Mill. He does not believe that the principle of rational benevolence dictates its own systematic application *de novo* in the project of a clean sweep of existing moral convictions. It should rather be used to support common-sense or intuitionist morality in general and to rectify it in detail. Moral reform should be 'positive and supplementary', not 'negative and destructive'.[57]

Also of interest is Sidgwick's anticipation of Moore, in his thesis that moral terms are indefinable. On this matter, unlike Moore, it is 'ought' and not 'good' whose indefinability he stresses. (Moore was prepared to define 'ought' in terms of 'good', in a way that makes Sidgwick's principle that a rational being ought to aim at good analytic, as 'more productive of good than any other possible action'.) From this it follows that even if, as Sidgwick believes, happiness, or 'desirable consciousness', is good 'it does not involve in its analysis any obligation to seek it.'[58]

It may be that part of Sidgwick's reason for thinking this is that, as he puts it, the judgement that something ought to be done, at least where the 'ought' in question is moral and categorical, carries with it 'an impulse or motive to action'.[59] But if, as most contemporary moral philosophers would maintain, the same practical implication is carried by the judgement that something is good (namely, that of bringing it into existence if it does not exist and of preserving it in existence if it does) there is no objection to a Moorean definition of 'ought' in terms of 'good', and Sidgwick's principle that one ought to aim at good is the tautology it surely appears to be.

Of Sidgwick's three main departures from classical utilitarianism, the first, that the principle that the happiness of all should be pursued needs to be supplemented with principles of distribution, is a reasonable enough criticism of Bentham and Mill. As was argued in the last section of the previous chapter, the treatment of the question at the end of Mill's book does not really take the measure of the problem. On the other hand, as it was further argued above, there are available to utilitarians arguments which seek to derive the intuitively acceptable principles of just distribution from the greatest happiness principle together with the law of diminishing marginal utility and other, more obviously factual, considerations about the inequality with which dis-utilities are distributed between men, by the circumstances in which they are placed or through the services they perform.

Secondly, the basic conflict that runs through Sidgwick's ethical reflections is an idiosyncratic version of an ancient pre-occupation of moral philosophers with the reconciliation of egoism and altruism. Where it has ordinarily been found difficult to explain how it is that men ought to pursue the good of all when they are psychologically so constituted so as to pursue only their own good, Sidgwick, denying that men always pursue their own good, if this is conceived as pleasure, as he thinks it should be, holds that it is self-evident that they *ought* to pursue both their own good and the good of all and that, despite a wide measure of coincidence, these two principles do at times have inconsistent implications. There must, surely, be something wrong here which is of a logical character and not merely an emotionally dissatisfying lack of harmony between our aspirations and the nature of things. Either the two principles are consistent (in accordance with the third of Sidgwick's criteria for axiomatic status) or one of them, at least, must be false. To those who believe in the overridingness of the moral 'ought' it will be the egoistic principle that one ought to aim at one's own good. Sidgwick's more elevated and dignified version of the clash between egoism and altruism, which represents it as a conflict between two equally rational convictions and not as one between selfish desire and impersonal reason, seems more readily resoluble than its more familiar analogue.

Sidgwick's theory of moral knowledge, finally, has little positive to commend it. Negatively, it has the merit of drawing attention to the indefiniteness of the classical utilitarians' account of the logical status of their fundamental principle. Is it analytic and true by definition or synthetic and substantive? If the latter, and thus, by reason of its generality, inductive could it possibly be strong enough to sustain the weight of the specific moral principles it is supposed to validate? It should be mentioned that many present-day critics of utilitarianism, particularly those who regard it as unable to accommodate our intuitive convictions about justice, distributive and retributive, appeal as he does to the self-evidence of the additional, independent principles they believe in. But for the most part they fail, as he with typical scrupulousness does not, to explain what sort of truth and justification such principles can aspire to.

(iii) F. H. BRADLEY

Bradley was, in his time, the most admired of the British idealists of the late nineteenth century. He was more imaginative and much more of a literary artist than T. H. Green, the founder of the school. Green had called on the philosophers of his generation to 'close up their Mill and Spencer' and, in his first work, *Ethical Studies* (1876), Bradley devoted a well-known chapter, the third, to the task of demolishing the ethics of 'pleasure for pleasure's sake'. There are two main themes in Bradley's critique of utilitarianism: one moral, the other logical. He invokes what he called 'the common moral consciousness', in other words conventionally edifying sentiment, to urge that utilitarianism is immoral and he borrowed an idea of Green's, that the ultimate end of conduct must be some kind of systematic whole to argue that the utilitarian *summum bonum* of the greatest happiness of all is a logical impossibility.

In seeking to show the immorality of utilitarianism Bradley says that he does not take common moral conviction to be unquestionably authoritative, but nevertheless he takes it, or a reflective version of it to be found in himself and his presumed readers, as a touchstone. In the first place, he says, happiness is not pleasure or a sum of pleasures. Secondly, the maximum pleasure of sentient beings is not the end of conduct. And neither, he goes on, is best achieved by deliberate pursuit. With something like Sidgwick's appeal to thoughtful intuition, he asks if the improvement of 'higher function', of virtue or perfection, at the cost of some increase of pain is not morally preferable to its opposite, an increase of pleasure accompanied by a deterioration of higher function. If anything is clear to the common moral consciousness it is that virtue, however much it may be a means to pleasure, is not good *because* it is such a means.

So far as there is argument here it is unpersuasive. The view that happiness is not definable in terms of pleasure derives its initial intuitive force from taking the word 'pleasure', irrelevantly, in its most elementary vernacular sense. The intuitive

93

falsity of the principle that pleasure is the ultimate good or end is dependent, as Sidgwick argued, on taking the pleasure involved to be that of the agent and ignoring the utilitarian requirement that it should be the pleasure of all sentient beings. Much the same is true of Bradley's claim that virtue does not owe its goodness to the fact, in so far as it is a fact, that virtue is a means to pleasure. Certainly utilitarians have hoped to show that virtue is a means to the agent's pleasure, in order to provide him with a motive for acquiring it, as well as to the pleasure of all. But it is to the second of these alone, according to them, that it owes its goodness. The contrast involved in his hypothesis about improvement of higher function at the expense of pleasure is one that a utilitarian, if consistent, should be disposed to question by saying that the state of affairs envisaged is one in which one source of human satisfaction is increased while another is diminished.

More definite and original is Bradley's crucial contention that the hedonistic end of the utilitarians is a logically impossible one. The end of conduct, he says, must be 'a definite unity', 'a concerete whole', it must be systematic. All that the utilitarians have to offer is 'an infinite, perishing series'. This seems an entirely arbitrary stipulation. A continuing income of £10,000 a year is just as proper an object of aspiration as the accumulation of a capital of £200,000 and the latter would be one way of getting the former and, indeed, be principally valuable on that account. It is not, of course, obvious in the least that the greatest happiness of sentient beings is an *infinite* series. There is good reason to suppose that eventually there will be no sentient life in the only part of the universe where we know it to exist, quite apart from the familiar immediate hazards to the human part of that life. On Bradley's own level of debate it could be argued that an infinity of quantities *can* have a sum anyway: $1 + \frac{1}{2} + \frac{1}{4} + \frac{1}{8} \ldots = 2$. But it is not so much the infinity as the 'perishing', temporal nature of the utilitarian end on which Bradley lays most stress.

About this criticism there are two points to be made. The first, subsequently made by Sidgwick in answer to Green's version of the objection, is that men are, after all, temporal beings who will need to realise value over the whole temporal extent of their lives and who will, therefore, quite rationally aim at doing so. This consideration can be reinforced by an *ad hominem* argument against the alternative account of the *summum bonum* Bradley offers in place of the general happiness. This is self-realisation. The self to be realised is not, of course, the actual self which, at any moment, is necessarily realised. It must be some sort of ideal self. But a self, even an ideal self, is still a temporal thing. If an achieved perfection of character could be thought to have a kind of timelessness it must still manifest itself in temporal items of conduct. In effect Bradley is maintaining that men should not seek to *produce* something, namely the greatest possible happiness for all, but rather to *be* something, let us say perfect. But it is not enough to attain perfection. It must be maintained and preserved. The non-temporal, non-serial realisation of an essentially temporal thing like the self is a much more 'wild and impossible fiction' than the utilitarian aim of the continuous maximisation of the greatest possible happiness.

The other point is perhaps less familiar. This is that Bradley's emphasis on the necessarily serial nature of pleasure betrays a vulgar identification of pleasure and pain with thrills and pangs. A common and fundamental object of human effort is fully satisfying employment in which the individual's powers are exercised to the limit. The achievement of this end is not a momentary kick, a climax of occupational ecstasy, but the attainment of a continuing state. Now the deep-seated and persistent desires whose satisfaction is the most important constituent of happiness are typically of this persistent kind. So, even conceived as a sum of pleasures, happiness is not of the crudely serial character that Bradley's criticism assumes.

One other objection Bradley deploys at some length to utilitarianism is that it requires the moral agent to act on probabilities, in holding that men ought to act in those ways which, experience has shown, will probably augment the general happiness. The result, he says, is that it replaces laws by rules. What he presumably means is that absolute specific principles of conduct are abandoned in favour of principles that can have exceptions. Warming to his theme, Bradley contends that, since each individual will have to judge for himself what the probable consequences of the alternatives before him are, there will ensue 'incessant practical casuistry'.[60] Why Bradley supposes that the individual's judgement on what the probable consequences of his action will be must be more wavering, subjective and wilful than his judgement of what it is his absolute obligation to do is not made clear. But it is, no doubt, true that a consequentialist manner of reasoning in morals leaves more scope for self-regarding distortion. On the other hand it also leaves more room for apt and effective altruism than a set of rigidly unconditional specific principles.

The example on which Bradley spends a good deal of time (do not commit adultery), is worth a little attention here. Used as it is in a criticism of Mill it may be thought to make a somewhat malicious allusion to Mill's association with Harriet Taylor, at a time when her first husband was still alive. That would not be so bad if it were not for the grotesque hypocrisy involved in Bradley's morally outraged posture on the subject. He may well have believed that Mill's relations with Mrs Taylor were literally adulterous, although this is now generally doubted. What is quite beyond doubt is that Bradley was himself an inveterate adulterer who for a long time spent a period each year with the wife of another man. His only moral achievement in this particular domain of human striving is that he managed to keep his misconduct from general notice. But it was not as champion of the principle 'do not be seen to commit adultery' that he rode forth so self-righteously against Mill.

On the point of philosophical substance, the chief defect of Bradley's handling of this example is lack of imagination or, at any rate, of concrete detail. Consider a standard type of late-Victorian situation. A cruel, but not certifiably insane, husband deserts his wife and children and fails to provide for them. Should a man who comes to love the abandoned wife and wishes to look after her be forbidden to live with her? Or take an actual case, that of George Eliot and George Henry Lewes. Lewes's wife had three illegitimate children by Thornton Leigh Hunt but, since Lewes had condoned the adultery when it first began, he could not get a divorce. Did his and George Eliot's long and deeply affectionate association therefore deserve moral censure? The most relaxed utilitarianism would not have sanctioned Bradley's own adulterous habit, since it involved no acceptance of continuing responsibility for the welfare of his mistress, but then it was not, as he must have supposed, representative of all forms of adulterous relationship.

Bradley handles Mill, in *Ethical Studies*, in a consistently sneering and contemptuous fashion, referring to him, for example, with abusive quotation-marks, as 'our great modern logician'. But in 1876 Mill had been safely dead for three years. In *Mr Sidgwick's Hedonism*, a pamphlet of 1877, whose subject was very much alive, his tone is much more moderate and cautious. For the most part he is content to repeat the arguments about the logical impossibility of the utilitarian end and its unacceptability to the ordinary moral consciousness which he had used against Mill. The force of these arguments is not diminished by the more reasonable mode in which they are expressed in the later work. Some additional points are made against particular details of Sidgwick's position. The rhetorical nature of Sidgwick's description as 'Reason' of the faculty of moral intuition to which he frequently appeals is brought out. Sidgwick's account of the practical, action-guiding force of reason is questioned. It should, rather, have been applauded as drawing attention to a problem many moral philosophers had evaded. Bradley accuses Sidgwick of repeating Mill's disastrous equivocation about the desirable, as that which is and ought to be desired, from an apparent inability to recall or notice Sidgwick's plain repudiation of psychological hedonism.

More interesting is his rejection of Sidgwick's account of ethical science. Sidgwick had held that a practical science of ethics could be derived from the principle of rational benevolence together with ordinary causal knowledge about the consequences for happiness of kinds of human action. Such a hope, Bradley maintains, is 'the mere dream of a doctrinaire'.[61] A true ethics, for Bradley, takes ordinary morality as given and seeks only to understand, not to alter it. It must, he thinks, inevitably conflict with ordinary morality but, since it has no practical aim, it will have no effect on actual conduct. This is a peculiar view, more than Wittgensteinian in its passivity in the face of an established 'form of life'. Philosophical ethics, for Bradley, must leave everything as it is. It hardly conforms to the position of those like Collingwood, who have attacked analytic philosophy for its indifference to the practical implications of philosophy and have contrasted it in this respect with the idealists. Morality and ethics, thus defined, must conflict and we are to act on the former. Is this because morality is truer than ethics? If so ethics becomes a pointless speculative game. If ethics is truer than morality why should we be guided by the latter? To the extent that ethics is speculative and intellectually experimental there are, indeed, good utilitarian reasons, set out at length by Sidgwick, for not reforming morality precipitately in accordance with its findings. But if it is a philosophical, and thus critical, investigation of morality, and not a neutral descriptive science of moral phenomena, it is absurd to rule out the idea that it could exercise an influence on the everyday moral thinking from which it arises and to which it is applied.

(iv) G. E. MOORE

G. E. Moore's *Principia Ethica* of 1903 has been by far the most influential criticism of utilitarian ethics. The purported refutation of ethical naturalism, which is the book's fundamental thesis, dominated moral philosophy for the first half of this century in Britain and, to a considerable extent, throughout the English-speaking world. It has, indeed, come to be based on very different grounds from those with which Moore provided it in the first chapter of his book but in any form it is, if sound, fatal to the most natural interpretation of utilitarianism.

Its essential claim is that judgements of value, and, in particular, moral judgements, cannot be taken to be, or to be strictly deducible from, statements of ordinary, natural, empirical fact, that can be established by the senses or introspection. Moore presented this as a thesis about the meaning of terms, holding that it is evident to inspection that no ethical term is identical in meaning to any term or collection of terms that serves to describe ordinary empirical facts. The conclusion he then drew was that judgements of value report unordinary, moral facts about an autonomous realm of values.

Since the 1930s Moore's successors have agreed with him about the difference between the evaluative and the empirical, that terms in the two domains are never synonymous and statements in them never logically equivalent, but for reasons very different from his. Developed antinaturalism holds that the lack of synonymy or equivalence that Moore detected expresses a deep-seated, underlying difference of function between utterances used to describe facts and utterances used to guide action. On this view judgements of value do not describe any facts at all, ordinary or unordinary. Their task is, rather, to give universal commands ('let everyone keep promises'), to express wishes ('would that everyone kept promises') or to give vent to emotions ('hurrah for promise-keeping'). Moore's own positive account of the nature of judgements of value, as statements of 'non-natural' fact, is thus the first casualty of the revised and improved version of the critical principle from which he originally derived it.

Moore's main discussion of utilitarianism is to be found in chapter 3 of *Principia Ethica*, 'Hedonism'. His first step is to argue that utilitarianism is really a naturalistic theory and so does fall within the scope of his proposed refutation of theories of that kind. One piece of evidence he draws on is that Sidgwick differed from the classical utilitarians in not supposing pleasure to be part of the definition of good, for he was compelled to base the hedonist principle on an intuition of which nothing is heard from Bentham and Mill. More directly to the point is Mill's statement that 'to think of an object as desirable (unless for the sake of its consequences) and to think of it as pleasant are one and the same thing'. In other words the concept of that which is desirable for its own sake and of that which is pleasant is a single concept or, again, 'desirable for its own sake' and 'pleasant' are identical in meaning. He goes on to diagnose the error he takes to be involved here, not very convincingly, as arising from the fact that the approval which it is the nature of value-judgements to express is a kind of liking, in other words a kind of pleasure.

Having thus firmly settled utilitarianism on the chopping-block of his polemical guillotine he proceeds to a more detailed examination of the arguments of Mill and Sidgwick. Against Mill he makes the rather well-worn, but still cogent, objections that Mill equivocates on the word 'desirable' and inconsistently abandons hedonism in his doctrine of different qualities of pleasure. More original are his arguments against the psychologically hedonist premise that pleasure alone is desired and the connected view that objects of desire that are apparently distinct from pleasure are either means to pleasure or, where the object in question is desired for its own sake, *parts* of pleasure or happiness.[62]

The theory that pleasure is the sole object of desire, he holds, is a confused misrepresentation of the truth that pleasure is always at least part of the cause of desire. The idea of drinking some wine occurs to one and causes an experience of pleasure. This actual, felt pleasure then, in its turn, causes a desire for a glass of wine to arise. What is desired is the wine, not the non-actual pleasure that is thought of in desiring it. Where pleasure comes in is as a consequence of the thought of the wine and as the cause of the desire for the wine.

The direct response to this objection has been given already in the discussion of Mill. The fact that a desire is for a glass of wine is perfectly compatible with its being also for pleasure, in particular the pleasure expected from drinking the glass of wine. The expected pleasure is the internal accusative of the desire. There is, of course, no such thing as desire for pleasure on its own, detached from any vehicle whatever, unless pleasure be taken, as in its most vernacular sense, as a label for a group of primitive, universal sources of satisfaction. It would, perhaps, have been better if Mill had said that pleasure is what is common to all objects of desire, rather than that pleasure alone is desired for its own sake. To expect pleasure from some conceived or imagined object is at least part of what differentiates the desire for it from its mere contemplation or envisagement.

There is something, in very general terms, in Moore's alternative thesis that actual pleasure is always some part of the cause of desire. This would seem to be true at least of acquired or learnt desires, as contrasted with instinctive ones. If, from politeness or curiosity, I eat a mysterious and unfamiliar-looking item from a tray of cocktail delicacies and find it pleasant this will foster a desire for an item of that kind for its own, gastronomic, sake next time I am offered one. Experiences of pleasure and pain are, platitudinously enough, the moulders of desire. But that is not to say, with Moore, that a desire is always attended with and immediately caused by a pleasant thought or the actual pleasure caused by the idea of some possibly available thing. For the most part desires are, or are attended by, unpleasant thoughts. That is, bluntly, why we try to satisfy them. Sometimes, when we have reason to think they are soon going to be satisfied, they may be pleasant. But when we think they may or probably will not be they are unpleasant. Even when they are pleasant we do not welcome their indefinite prolongation.

Moore becomes distinctly heated when he turns to Mill's account of the way in which things that are originally desired as means to pleasure, like virtue or, in his somewhat unfortunate analogous case, money, come to be desired for their own sakes, by the truly conscientious man and the miser, respectively. Mill says that such objects change from being means to happiness into 'parts of happiness'. Moore describes this as 'contemptible nonsense'.[63] A man who desires money desires coins and banknotes. Does Mill really mean that solid material objects are literally parts of a mental state like happiness? Thinking of this degree of plainness could appeal only to a corruptly sophisticated taste for the primitive. Anyone who, for such a reason, could not make head or tail of the remark that a man's family or house or business is a great part of his happiness should move into some more practical line of work than philosophy. It would be insulting to Moore's intelligence to suppose that he was really unable to distinguish between the satisfaction one man gets from virtue, which is by way of the good opinion it causes other people to have of him, and that of another, which comes directly from the exercise of virtue, whether anyone else knows about it or not.

Moore wrote of Sidgwick: 'His personality did not attract me, and I found his lectures rather dull. From his published works, especially, of course, his *Methods of Ethics*, I have gained a good deal. . . .'[64] The aspect of Sidgwick's thought of which he is most critical in *Principia Ethica* is its insistence that ultimate good or value is only to be found in the conscious states of a sentient being. Against Sidgwick's conclusion that experienced pleasure is the only thing that is ultimately good Moore develops his thought-experiment about the two worlds, one entirely beautiful, the other entirely repellent and ugly, with regard to which it is guaranteed that no 'human being has or ever, by any possibility, *can*, live in either, can ever see and enjoy the beauty of the one or hate the foulness of the other'.[65]

Moore maintains that it is intuitively self-evident to him that it would be good for the beautiful but unexperienceable world to exist and bad for the ugly one to exist. If the guarantee that neither world can ever be experienced is acceptable, it might seem more rational to prefer that the ugly one should exist, both as a safe dumping-ground for the ugliness that composes it and because it would be a deplorable misuse of resources to waste beauty by sequestering it from any possibility of being enjoyed in the way the hypothesis proposes. In fact, the guarantee is not very acceptable, either psychologically or logically. Can the barrier be proof against all ingenuity of intrusion? If God is the contractor employed in the construction will it not coarsen him, to our long-run disadvantage, if he is commissioned to run up an entirely repulsive world? On the logical point, if the guarantee that the world in question cannot be experienced is more than contingent does it even make sense to suppose that the world exists?

Moore goes on to inquire whether it is pleasure alone or rather the consciousness of pleasure that Sidgwick holds to be the supreme good. He says that 'it is far more possible that we should some day be able to produce the intensest pleasure, without any consciousness that it is there, than that we should be able to produce mere colour, without its being any particular colour'.[66] Many philosophers who hold that pleasure and pain are mental states of which we are infallibly aware and which necessarily intimate themselves to us would deny that there is any difference between Moore's two cases. Both, they would say, involve self-contradiction. If pleasure and consciousness of it can be coherently distinguished, Sidgwick, as Moore realises, would take the latter to be the ultimate good. Unconscious pleasure could still be significant because of its causal relations to conscious pleasure and pain. One might say that a man derived unconscious pleasure from the prevalence of an easy and amicable atmosphere in his family circle, if, for instance, it was such a normal condition as to escape his attention. It would still be preferable to the unconscious pain produced by a persistently disagreeable atmosphere because of the different effects of these subliminal emotional backgrounds on the hedonic quality of the experiences of which he is conscious.

Finally Moore addresses himself to the question of whether consciousness of pleasure is the ultimate good. Allowing that anything that is ultimately good may *contain* consciousness of pleasure, he denies that its goodness is constituted by the consciousness of pleasure it contains. That which is a necessary condition of goodness need not be good in isolation. There is a quite persuasive argument here which Moore does not develop. J. J. C. Smart has considered the hypothesis of man sitting in a machine which continuously supplies him with intense and exquisite sensations of pleasure.[67] Is this the ideal mode of life for the whole sentient creation? The practical objections to this hypothesis are obvious. Would any exquisite sensation remain exquisite if it went on all the time? Who would keep the machines in working order and, indeed, ensure that their occupants were maintained in sufficient biological working order for them to be sensitive to pleasure? Feats of technological imagination are called for here about the reliability of automatic operation of the pleasure machines which depart rather massively from our experience of household gadgets. If the feats are performed we are confronted with an ethical analogue of Descartes' demon which is as well calculated to undermine the thesis that pleasure is what is ultimately good as the demon is to undermine belief in the overall reliability of our cognitive faculties.

In considering the view that consciousness of pleasure alone, or 'in isolation', is the only ultimate good Moore draws another distinction with much the same logical fragility as that between pleasure and consciousness of it. The possession of pleasure by persons, he says, is not the same thing as the existence of that quantity of pleasure. At first he seems to be envisaging the possibility of altogether unowned pleasure. Even if this were a coherent notion it would have little practical import since there is no way in which intentional human action could affect it. However, it seems clear that it is not coherent. Pleasure is an essentially relational idea. For pleasure to occur an experient must take pleasure in something he is experiencing. But, as the discussion proceeds, it appears, rather, that what Moore is concerned with is the way in which a given amount of pleasure is distributed between different people. He does not pick out this problem, considered above in Chapter 3, section (v), clearly enough to make any useful contribution to it.

On the whole, then, Moore's specific arguments against utilitarianism, where they depart from the familiar points about desirability and Mill's theory of different qualities of pleasure, do not amount to much. The real force of his critique, and its actual effectiveness, must be attributed to his general argument against naturalism. I have examined this at length elsewhere.[68] If, as I argue there, the pleasantness of a thing is an intrinsic, non-contingent reason for pursuing it, then the practicality of moral judgements, which it is the residual element of truth in Moore's antinaturalism to stress, is not merely something with which utilitarianism is consistent (and not, as he thinks, the rock on which it comes to grief), it is also something which is more adequately catered for by utilitarianism than by any other ethical theory.

V. EPILOGUE: CONTEMPORARY UTILITARIANISM

Since Moore's *Principia Ethica* moral philosophy, at least in Britain and to a large extent in the English-speaking world, has passed through three phases. In the first Moore's own combination of a consequentialist theory of right action with an intuitionist account of the indefinable property of goodness prevailed. Because of its definition of rightness in terms of consequences it was sometimes called 'ideal utilitarianism'. But, given the strenuousness of Moore's opposition to hedonism, the label is less naturally applicable to him than to the position of Rashdall, set out in his thorough and judicious *Theory of Good and Evil* (1907), a book superior to Moore's by reason of its author's notably greater capacity to understand, and, indeed, actual knowledge of, the history of ethical speculation. Rashdall includes pleasure, along with knowledge and virtue, among the ideal ends of conduct. The Moorean view was given a brilliantly concise expression in Russell's 'The Elements of Ethics' (four essays first published in 1910 and brought together in his *Philosophical Essays* of that year). But two years later Santayana's essay 'Hypostatic Ethics', in *Winds of Doctrine*, converted Russell to a theoretically rather inarticulate subjectivism from which he at length emerged in 1954 to the qualified, tentative utilitarianism of Part One of *Human Society in Ethics and Politics*.

Between H. A. Prichard's 'Does Moral Philosophy Rest on a Mistake?' in 1912 and W. D. Ross's *Foundations of Ethics* in 1939 the prevailing academic ethical theory was one which rejected the consequentialism in which Moore had agreed with the utilitarians while accepting his intuitionist account of moral knowledge. For Prichard and his school it is the obligatoriness of action that is revealed to intuition, not the goodness of ends, and the intuitions in question are general in form, asserting the rightness of actions of a kind and not that of particular actions. Along with Kant's, of which it is a less provocatively rationalistic version, this is, of all ethical theories, that which is furthest in spirit from the doctrine of Bentham and Mill. In its pristine form it is open to the objection that the specific absolute obligations it claims we intuit are liable to conflict. Prichard's remedy was a theoretical epicycle. As well as intuitions of duty he held that there are intuitions of comparative stringency as between conflicting duties, an uncomfortable departure from the principle of the absoluteness of obligation which he was anxious to sustain. Ross, more consistently, took intuitions of duty to be only *'prima facie'*, to discover no more than that kinds of action *tend* to be right. To adjudicate in cases of conflict he called upon the plainly consequentialist principle that one ought always to produce as much good as possible.

In the third phase, which has not long been concluded, Moore's anti-naturalism was reaffirmed on more secure foundations, namely as a consequence of the intrinsically practical, action-guiding nature of judgements of value. The emotivism of Stevenson and the prescriptivism of Hare, in agreeing that value-judgements are not statements, true or false, and thus not possible items of knowledge, lumped utilitarianism and Moore's own positive theory together in the limbo of error. According to these theories ultimate values are chosen, not discovered. The only constraints imposed on the valuer are personal sincerity and formal universality in the expression of his convictions. There can, on such views, be no objective restriction to the ends of morality. They can be of any concrete character whatever, provided that they are sincerely and impersonally affirmed. The reaction against this ethics of pure choice was initiated by the irresistible re-emergence of the idea that morality does have a specific content, that the moral character of an action is necessarily bound up with its effects in the way of harm or injury to others.

J. J. C. Smart, in his *Outlines of A Utilitarian System of Ethics* (1961), neatly reconciles his own commitment to a utilitarian morality with admission of the validity of prescriptivist ethics. He acknowledges that the fundamental utilitarian principle is not a true or false proposition, but is rather a basic moral resolution, which is not amenable to proof. But, he says, he embraces it as his fundamental moral choice and supposes that it will recommend itself to any benevolent person. What, after all, is benevolence but the steady pursuit of the happiness of all? Of course, for those who do not wish or choose to be benevolent, his subsequent development of the details of a utilitarian morality can at best be of theoretical interest. This is less powerful an *ad hominem* argument than he supposes. Few would blithely reject altogether the choice of a benevolent style of conduct. But the serious, controversial issue is as to whether benevolence is enough, whether it is the whole of virtue. One disposed to choose the regularian style of morality associated with an ethics like Prichard's would reply that, while all in favour of benevolence, he was even more concerned to be just. Smart's ingenious rhetoric really evades the fundamental point at issue.

In 1936, when utilitarianism must have been at its lowest ebb, R. F. Harrod, in an essay, 'Utilitarianism Revised', proposed a modification to the doctrine of Bentham and Mill, at least in its usual interpretation, which has become a major topic of ethical discussion in the last two decades. Harrod proposed a remedy for what he admitted to be the defects of the utilitarian theory of obligation, its representation of what the ordinary moral consciousness takes to be hard and fast laws by rules of thumb, always liable to suspension in particular cases. Instead of defining the wrongness of an action in terms of its effects, he defined it in terms of the effects of a general practice of performing actions of that kind in relevantly similar circumstances.

The idea that considerations of utility could support the acceptance and observance of rules had been in circulation at least since Hume. Rules could be argued for in this way as required for swift action in emergencies and to establish security of expectations. But the idea that rightness should be defined directly in terms of the utility of rules, from which the rightness of particular acts would then be derivative, seemed new. J. O. Urmson, however, argued in his essay 'The Intepretation of the Moral Philosophy of J. S. Mill' (1953) that rule-utilitarianism was Mill's own position. Mill defined the rightness of actions in terms of their *tendency* to augment the general happiness. But a particular action cannot have a tendency, only a class of actions can. (Harrod had noted that such a view might be implicit in the classical texts but said that, if it was, it needed to be brought into the open.)

In the last ten years this has been the most closely examined aspect of utilitarianism. Smart, in his *Outlines* and elsewhere, has been the most fervent of those who hold that to the extent that rule-utilitarianism enjoins different conduct from its act-utilitarian alternative, the latter is self-evidently to be preferred. To follow the former would involve a loss of attainable utility and would thus be irrational rule-worship. On the other side R. B. Brandt has been an equally persistent defender of the rule-utilitarian position. The latest and most authoritative expression of his views is in his 'Toward a Credible Form of Utilitarianism' (1963).

The debate was raised to a new level of refinement and precision in David Lyon's powerful monograph *Forms and Limits of Utilitarianism* (1965). Elaborating an array of distinctions which contribute to a clearer understanding of all aspects of utilitarianism, he argues that simple or traditional utilitarianism and what he calls general utilitarianism, which holds that an action ought to be done if and only if the doing of actions of that kind in relevantly similar circumstances would make the largest contribution to utility, necessarily enjoin the very same things. What makes the circumstances of one action of the kind in question relevantly similar to those of another are just those which affect the resulting utility, for good or ill. If keeping my promise here and now will produce less utility than breaking it, my duty to keep it cannot be established in the face of this fact by the utility of promise-keeping in general, since all the many cases in which promise-keeping is the most utility-producing action are relevantly different from the present case just in respect of their productiveness of utility.

Lyons distinguishes rule-utilitarianism proper from the generalised utilitarianism he has shown to be equivalent in its particular injunctions to act-utilitarianism of the traditional kind. The doctrine that an action is right if and only if it conforms to a set of rules general acceptance of which would maximise utility (Lyons's formula for what he calls 'ideal rule-utilitarianism') is a genuine and substantive alternative to act-utilitarianism and its generalised equivalent. But, he concludes, this substantive rule-utilitarianism gets the worst of both worlds. On the one hand it is less calculated to maximise utility than act-utilitarianism; on the other it is as much exposed as act-utilitarianism to the objections about the inadequacy of utilitarianism to sustain intuitively required principles of justice and fairness.

The two foregoing paragraphs give only the barest sketch of the content of Lyons's book. Although its final upshot is unfavourable to utilitarianism, that verdict is passed on utilitarianism as a *total* account of rational moral thinking. In contrast to the complete dismissal of utilitarianism that prevailed during what may be called the period of anti-naturalism, it is now widely conceded that at least a large and central segment of rational moral thinking is utilitarian in character. The crucial issue is the one that Mill failed to confront effectively in the last chapter of his book, that of whether the principle of utility must be supplemented by a principle, or principles, of comparable generality if it is to make good its claim to be a rational reconstruction of moral thinking.

NOTES

In page references to the works of Bentham and Mill the following abbreviations are used:

H W. Harrison (ed.), Jeremy Bentham: *A Fragment on Government and An Introduction to the Principles of Morals and Legislation* (Oxford, 1948).

E John Stuart Mill, *Utilitarianism, Liberty and Representative Government* (Everyman edition, London, 1910).

W M. Warnock (ed.), *Utilitarianism* (London, 1962).

1. Bentham, *Introduction to the Principles of Morals and Legislation (I.P.M.L.)*, ch. 1, para. 2. *H.* p. 126. *W.* p. 34.
2. Bentham, *I.P.M.L.* ch. 1, para. 6. *H.* p. 127. *W.* p. 35.
3. Bentham, *I.P.M.L.* ch. 1, para. 4. *H.* p. 126. *W.* p. 35.
4. Mill, *Utilitarianism (U.)*, ch. 2. *E.* p. 6. *W.* p. 257.
5. Bentham, *I.P.M.L.* ch. 1, para. 10. *H.* p. 127. *W.* p. 36.
6. Bentham, *I.P.M.L.* ch. 1, para 1. *H.* p. 125. *W.* p. 33.
7. Mill, *U.* ch. 4. *E.* p. 35. *W.* p. 292.
8. Mill, *U.* ch. 4. *E.* p. 36. *W.* p. 292.
9. Hobbes, *Leviathan*, ed. Pogson Smith (Oxford, 1909), part 1, ch. 6, p. 41.
10. Cf. *British Moralists*, ed. Raphael, vol. 1, 'Hobbes to Gay' (Oxford, 1969), pp. 104–18.
11. Hume, *Treatise of Human Nature* (ed. Selby-Bigge, Oxford, 1888), Book III, part 1, sec. 1, p. 457.
12. Ibid. Book III, part 1, sec. 1, p. 469.
13. Ibid. Book III, part 1, sec. 1, pp. 468–9.
14. Ibid. Book III, part 1, sec. 2, p. 471.
15. Ibid. Book III, part 2, sec. 1, p. 481.
16. Ibid. Book III, part 3, sec. 1, p. 576.
17. Ibid. Book III, part 3, sec. 1, p. 581.
18. Beccaria, *On Crimes and Punishments*, trans. H. Paolucci (New York, 1963).
19. Hume, *Treatise*, Book III, part 2, sec. 1, p. 482.
20. E. A. Burtt (ed.), *The English Philosophers from Bacon to Mill* (New York, 1939), p. 773.

21. Ibid. p. 774.

22. Paley, *Principles of Moral and Political Philosophy* (London, 1785), Book 1, ch. 7, p. 36.

23. Bentham, *Introduction to the Principles of Morals and Legislation*, preface, para. 7. H. p. 119.

24. Ibid. ch. 1, para. 1, footnote 1. H. p. 125. W. p. 33.

25. Ibid. ch. 17, part 1, 'The Limits between Private Ethics and the Art of Legislation'. H. pp. 410–23.

26. Ibid. ch. 17, part 1, para. 19. H. p. 422.

27. Ibid. ch. 17, part 1, para. 19. H. p. 423.

28. Ibid. ch. 1, para. 11. H. p. 128. W. p. 36.

29. Ibid. ch. 1, para. 12. H. p. 128. W. p. 36.

30. Ibid. ch. 1, para. 13. H. p. 128. W. p. 36.

31. Ibid. ch. 1, para. 14.4. H. p. 130. W. p. 38.

32. Ibid. ch. 2, para. 19. H. p. 146. W. p. 58.

33. Ibid. ch. 4, para. 3. H. pp. 151–2. W. pp. 64–5.

34. Ibid. ch. 7, para. 1. H. p. 189.

35. Ibid. ch. 17, part 1, para. 7. H. p. 413.

36. Ibid. ch. 12, para. 34, footnote. H. p. 280.

37. Mill, *On Liberty*, ch. 1. E. p. 74. W. p. 136.

38. Mill, *Utilitarianism*, ch. 2. E. p. 7. W. pp. 258–9.

39. Cf. G. H. von Wright, *The Varieties of Goodness* (London, 1963) chs 4 and 5.

40. *Values and Intentions* (Stanford, 1969). pp. 33–8.

41. Mill, *Utilitarianism*, ch. 3. E. p. 25. W. p. 280.

42. Ibid. ch. 3. E. p. 26. W. p. 281.

43. Ibid. ch. 3. E. p. 28. W. p. 283.

44. Ibid. ch. 1. E. p. 4. W. pp. 254–5.

45. Ibid. ch. 1. E. p. 4. W. p. 255.

46. Ibid. ch. 4. E. p. 35. W. p. 292.

47. Ibid. ch. 4. E. p. 36. W. p. 293.

48. Ibid. ch. 4. E. p. 26. W. p. 293.

49. Cf. *The Ground and Nature of the Right* (New York, 1955), ch. 1.

50. Cf. A. Quinton, 'The Bounds of Morality', in *Ethics and Social Justice*, ed. H. E. Kiefer and M. Munitz (Albany, 1970).

51. Cf. D. H. Monro, *Empiricism and Ethics* (1967), part 3.

52. Mill, *Utilitarianism*, ch. 5. E. pp. 54–5. W. pp. 314–15.

53. Hume, *Treatise of Human Nature*, Book III, part 2, sec. 1, p. 482.

54. H. Sidgwick, *The Methods of Ethics*, Book 1, ch. 3, sec. 3 (6th edn, London, 1901), pp. 31–5.

55. Ibid. Book III, ch. 11, sec. 2, pp. 338–43.

56. Ibid. Book III, ch. 13, sec. 3, pp. 379–84.

57. Ibid. Book IV, ch. 5.
58. C. D. Broad, *Five Types of Ethical Theory* (London, 1930), p. 145.
59. Sidgwick, op. cit. Book I, ch. 3, sec. 3, p. 34.
60. F. H. Bradley, *Ethical Studies* (Oxford, 1876), Essay 3, p. 109.
61. F. H. Bradley, *Collected Essays* (Oxford, 1935), p. 113.
62. G. E. Moore, *Principia Ethica* (Cambridge, 1903), ch. 3, sec. 42, pp. 68–71.
63. Ibid. ch. 3, sec. 43, p. 72.
64. P. Schilpp (ed.), *The Philosophy of G. E. Moore* (Evanston, 1942), p. 16.
65. G. E. Moore, op. cit. ch. 3, sec. 50, p. 84.
66. Ibid. ch. 3, sec. 52, p. 89.
67. J. J. C. Smart, *An Outline of a System of Utilitarian Ethics* (Melbourne, 1961), pp. 11–14.
68. *The Nature of Things* (London, 1973), ch. 12.

BIBLIOGRAPHY

I. Histories

Leslie Stephen, *The English Utilitarians*, 3 volumes (London, 1900).

Ernest Allbee, *A History of English Utilitarianism* (New York, 1902).

Élie Halévy, *The Growth of Philosophic Radicalism*, trans. M. Morris (London, 1928).

John Plamenatz, *The English Utilitarians* (Oxford, 1949).

II. The Precursors

Richard Cumberland, *De Legibus Naturae*, 1672. Selections with parallel translation in D. D. Raphael (ed.), *British Moralists 1650–1800*, vol. I, pp. 77–102 (Oxford, 1969).

John Gay, *Dissertation Concerning the Fundamental Principle of Virtue or Morality* (London, 1731): prefixed to Archbishop King's *Essay on the Origin of Evil*. Reprinted in E. A. Burtt (ed.), *The English Philosophers from Bacon to Mill* (New York, 1939).

David Hume, *Treatise of Human Nature*, Book III (London, 1740). *Enquiry Concerning the Principles of Morals* (London, 1751). Cf. V. C. Chappell (ed.), *Hume: a collection of critical essays*, pp. 240–334 (Garden City, N.Y., 1966; London, 1968).

Abraham Tucker, *The Light of Nature Pursued*, by 'Edward Search' (1768–78).

William Paley, *The Principles of Moral and Political Philosophy* (1785).

III. The Main Texts

Jeremy Bentham, *Introduction to the Principles of Morals and Legislation* (1789). Edited by W. Harrison, with *A Fragment on Government* (Oxford, 1948). Cf. David Baumgardt, *Bentham and the Ethics of Today* (Princeton, N.J., 1952). A. J. Ayer, 'The Principle of Utility', in *Philosophical Essays* (London, 1954). H. L. A. Hart, 'Bentham', in *Proceedings of the British Academy*, vol. 48 (Oxford, 1962).

James Mill, *A Fragment on Mackintosh* (London, 1835).

John Stuart Mill, *Utilitarianism* (London, 1863). (There are many subsequent editions.) Cf. Karl Britton, *John Stuart Mill*, chap. 2 (Harmondsworth, 1953). J. B. Schneewind (ed.), *Mill: A Collection of Critical Essays*, pp. 145–250 (Garden City, N.Y., 1968; London, 1969). Alan Ryan, *The Philosophy of John Stuart Mill*, chaps 11 and 12 (London, 1970).

IV. Nineteenth-Century Criticism and Development

John Grote, *An Examination of the Utilitarian Philosophy* (Cambridge, 1870).

Henry Sidgwick, *The Methods of Ethics* (London, 1874).

F. H. Bradley, *Ethical Studies*, chap. 3 (Oxford, 1876).

G. E. Moore, *Principia Ethica*, chap. 3 (Cambridge, 1903).

V. Contemporary Writings

R. F. Harrod, 'Utilitarianism Revised', in *Mind*, vol. 45 (1936) pp. 137–56.

J. J. C. Smart, *Outlines of a Utilitarian System of Ethics* (Melbourne, 1961).

David Lyons, *Forms and Limits of Utilitarianism* (Oxford, 1965).

Jan Narveson, *Morality and Utility* (Baltimore, 1967).

D. H. Hodgson, *Consequences of Utilitarianism* (Oxford, 1967).

ıchael D. Bayles (ed.), *Contemporary Utilitarianism* (Garden City, N.Y., 1968).

Cf. also the following works, which are of a broadly utilitarian tendency.

W. T. Stace, *The Concept of Morals* (London and New York, 1937).

Moritz Schlick, *Problems of Ethics* (trans. D. Rynin) (New York, 1939). (1st German edition, *Fragen der Ethik*, 1930.)

C. I. Lewis, *Analysis of Knowledge and Valuation*, Book III (La Salle, Illinois, 1946).

——*The Ground and Nature of the Right* (New York, 1955).

——*Values and Imperatives* (Stanford, California, 1969).